JOACHIM MASANNEK

The Wild Soccer Bunch

Translated from the German by Helga Schier

Editor: Michael Part

Original title: Die Wilden Fussballkerle. Julie die Viererkette.
Baumhaus Verlag in the Bastei Luebbe Gmbh & Co. KG
© 2010 by Bastei Luebbe GmbH & Co. KG, Cologne
"Die Wilden Fußballkerle"™ und © dreammotion GmbH

Special thanks to:
Yonatan, Yaron, and Guy Ginsberg

Library of Congress Cataloging-in-Publication data in file.

ISBN 978-0-9844257-6-1

Published by Sole Books

First Edition August 2012
Printed in the United States of America

Layout: Lynn M. Snyder

10 9 8 7 6 5 4 3 2 1

RMA584DR939, September, 2012

Hi *Wild Soccer Bunch* fans!

You are holding the fourth book in the *Wild Soccer Bunch* series. I know how many of you were waiting for this moment and I'm glad that each book makes you ask for more!

In soccer, as in life, great achievements are a result of group effort. Every great player will tell you that they are only as good as their team. The secret to your own success is to trust your teammates and to treat everyone as you would like to be treated. It is easy to blame your teammates for the losses and errors they make. But this won't help your team improve or win. Only true friendship and trust will bring you back when things aren't going well. In order to trust your teammates, you need to know them, like a family. The more you know and like your teammates, the better you understand each other and the better you will play. To get to know each other better, you must spend time together, practice, and build your trust, communication skills, and appreciation for each other.

I wish you a great soccer year.

Your Friend and Teammate,

Landon Donovan

JOACHIM MASANNEK

The Wild Soccer Bunch

Book 4

Julian the Mighty

Illustrations by Jan Birck

Sole
BOOKS

TABLE OF CONTENTS

The Twilight Zone

Shhh! Now be real quiet!

Do you hear it?

Silence. Not a sound. No wind. No animal. Nothing. Listen to it.

That's my world; the world of Julian Fort Knox, the all-in-one defender. I know, long name. Everyone says so, but after the adventures unfold in this tale, the pain and suffering, the terror and the joy, more will change than just my long name.

But beware! Better look for a safe place to hide, just in case! Best you stand with your back to the wall and always carry a flashlight. This story will take you on a tightrope walk over a deep and dark abyss, and like a coin, this story has two totally different sides. One side promises adventure and happiness. Like when you face your fears. The other side is failure and misery. Like when you risk it all and don't listen to the fear in your heart that warns you. It's hard to tell the two apart. Believe me, I know.

I tossed the coin up in the air one more time. It spun so fast it made me dizzy. Then it dropped against a twig, changed direction, and landed on the ruins of the old house gate that towered over me, dark and threatening.

Lying on my back in the Grim Woods, flashlight in hand and head resting on the moss, I looked up into the sky and watched the stars make room for the morning light. The stars sparkled one last time as if they were coins lit by my flashlight.

I took a deep breath and spread my arms as wide as I could. Then I closed my eyes, exhaled slowly and tried to feel which side of the coin I belonged to, which side I came from.

To my left was the Green Forest – that's the world of the *Wild Soccer Bunch* and my mother. To my right were the area known as "The Projects" with a huge empty lot we called the "Prairie" and at the other end of the prairie, the ominous "Graffiti Towers" that loomed over and pointed into the sky, darkening the morning down below. Mickey the bulldozer and his *Unbeatables* lived in these uninviting steel and concrete building projects. So did my father. I was sure of that.

But nobody dared to go there. Not on purpose, anyway. Even the Grim Woods, as we called the forest separating our world from the "Projects," was forbidden. But yet, here I was and no one knew I was here. It was my secret. My mom always said, "you are only as sick as your secrets." Well, this was my biggest secret which is probably why I didn't feel too well about being here. I came here just before dawn, just before the birds started their singing for the day, greeting the sun, when all that is goodness in the city was still sleeping.

I thought I was alone.

But that day I was wrong.

I heard the footsteps too late because I had been lost in thought. I jumped up as a gang of kids broke through the brush and came directly towards me. I could see their shadows between the trees, but they hadn't seen me. I looked around; too late to run away. Where could I hide? The trees around me were half dead spruce. No branches within reach. The only hiding place in sight was the old house ruins.

Without hesitation I climbed the gate and flattened myself on the archway. The stones moaned and groaned, and I prayed they'd hold my weight. Thank God they did.

Anxious, I stared at the creatures approaching from the Grim Woods. I knew it! It was Mickey the bulldozer, the Darth Vader of our neighborhood. His breath rattled like the chains of two dozen medieval torturers. His eyes glowed like killer satellites. His t-shirt stretched like a balloon over his enormous belly and the gobs of muscles and the dark soul underneath. Just like sugar attracts flies, Mickey the bulldozer attracts morons, and his gang, the *Unbeatables,* who were now decidedly beatable, followed him everywhere: Oscar Octopus, Mow-Down Mark, Juggernaut Jim, Humungous Henry, Rick the Grim Reaper and Kong, the monumental creature from the Prairie of Mongolia. We all knew that these jerks didn't care about soccer any more, but what I was about to learn was above and beyond anything any of us had ever imagined. They were a band of thieves! If any of them ever played in a movie, it would be a bad horror movie.

They laughed and jeered as they marched through the Grim Woods. Candy, comic books, and soda cans fell from their plastic bags, but they didn't care. They had plenty, enough to supply all the children's birthday parties for centuries to come.

Suddenly Mickey stopped. He stood directly below me and told his gang to shut up. They did, and expectantly they surrounded their leader. Mickey the bulldozer grinned, grabbed a coke, opened it, gulped it down, crushed the can between his fingers, and then lifted his arms to the sky: "Yeah! That's how you do it!"

He burped as loud as a foghorn and the others doubled over, laughing. Then they drank and lifted their arms in unison and yelled: "That's how we do it!"

Then they all burped.

I had to grin. But my grin disappeared in a heartbeat when I accidentally bumped my flashlight, which rolled towards the edge of the archway. If it fell, it would hit Mickey smack on the head. OMG! That would be it for me. I'm sure they had plenty of putrid ideas of how to dispose of an all-in-one defender!

Just before the flashlight was about to fall over the edge, I reached out and grabbed it at the very last second. Unfortunately, a few little stones came loose and

rained down on Mickey.

Boink boink boink! They hit his head, and boink, the last little stone landed on his nose just as he looked up at the archway, directly above him.

"Hey!" he yelled at the others. "Shut up for a sec."

They were quiet in no time and just as fast, their eyes scanned up searching for the source of the noise. Luckily, I had flattened myself as much as possible and pushed my face into the stone. My heart beat like rolling thunder, and Mickey's next words hit me like lightning.

"Octopus!" he barked. "Something moved up there."

Octopus, the skinny jerk with a Mohawk, and arms so long I swear they touched the ground, did as he was told immediately.

I gave up. This was it. The end. Finito. But then I saw the coin that had fallen into the ruins. It was crooked and all rusty, but it was still my lucky coin. I had found it years ago on the train tracks near my house on Dearborn Street and had carried it with me ever since. In fact, I carried a lot of stuff around in my pockets. That's why they were all torn up and ragged, and my mom was always upset with me. She had no idea what this "junk" was good for. She had no idea about the double life of her own all-in-one defender. And if I didn't come up with a brilliant idea soon, she would find out, and that would lead to all kinds of trouble!

Octopus began to climb up the gate like a giant octopus slithering out of the primordial seas searching for something to eat.

I stared at my lucky coin as if it was the Philosopher's Stone. Then I had an idea: I had a foxtail that once belonged to my father. And the foxtail was exactly what I needed.

I carefully turned to my side and rummaged in my pockets. OMG! Where was it? Octopus came closer and closer. Eight, no seven more seconds and he'd be ... phew, there it was. I felt the soft fur, pulled it out, and inched towards the lucky coin. I could see Octopus' hand reaching the top of the arch, looking for something to hold on to.

Oh man, I had to move fast. I waved and wiggled the foxtail near the edge of the archway, but Mickey didn't notice, and Octopus was about to pull himself up so he didn't see it either. I had no choice. I kissed my lucky coin one last time and threw it down at Mickey. It hit him on the top of his fat head.

"Hey!" he complained. "What was that?"

He fished the coin from his matted hair, looked at it, grumbled, and then lifted his eyes towards the archway, where he finally saw the foxtail.

"Pssst! Come on down, Octopus!" he hissed trying to keep his voice low. "It's just a squirrel." Luckily, the jerk had failed biology and couldn't tell the difference between a fox and a squirrel.

"Excellent!" I thought. "Now lose yourself!" But unfortunately Octopus was not that smart either, and it took him a while to react. His Mohawk appeared above the rim, then his oily forehead. I clenched my teeth and prepared myself for his eyes inching above the rim and noticing me. But suddenly the moron stopped moving, and not a moment too soon. Phew! The connection between Octopus' brain, arms, and legs had finally made their synapse!

"Why didn't you say so?" He complained to his leader, and it had been so long Mickey had almost forgotten what they were talking about, then he remembered and he laughed.

"Come on, forget it. The cute little squirrel paid for your troubles. Here!"

He tossed my lucky coin to Octopus. Octopus caught it and jumped down from the gate.

"Are you kidding me? This isn't worth anything!" he complained as he turned the grimy coin over between his fingers. He was right; it was just an old Buffalo nickel. It meant nothing to anyone but me.

"Whatever. If you have a problem with it, complain to the squirrel!" Mickey mocked him.

For a moment Octopus seemed to actually consider this option. My heart skipped a beat. Was the jerk really going to climb back up the archway to complain to a foxtail that was pretending to be a squirrel? But then the dim bulb grew a little brighter and burned through the cobwebs, and he understood the uselessness of such an endeavor. Octopus shook his head and tossed the coin into the forest.

"Let's go!" Mickey hurried his gang along. "Party time! Or are you planning to give away the candy in your pockets?"

Laughing and jeering, the *Unbeatables* left the Grim Woods and marched on toward the empty lot everyone called "The Prairie." On the other side of it, the ominous Graffiti Towers loomed large.

I took a deep breath, and pinched myself three times before I was sure that I was still alive. Holy guacamole! A lot of time had passed. The birds were already awake, so I jumped off the gate and flew home as fast as I could.

Hot Chocolate and Big Secrets

My mother and my little brother, Josh, were up already.
In the kitchen at 44 Dearborn Street, the smell of coffee
and hot chocolate drifted through the air. Adding the
breakfast rolls I bought on my way home, our breakfast
was perfect. Oh, I was so glad and happy to have a
brother, a mother, and a home. Really. I was. You have
to believe me, or I won't continue to tell you this story.
We clear on that?

Good! Glad we agree. But you must swear an oath.
So close the book, put your hand onto the *Wild Soccer
Bunch* logo, and repeat after me:
"I believe that Julian
Fort Knox, the all-in-
one defender, loves
his mother, his
brother, and his home,
with all his heart."

Go on! What are you waiting for? Close the book already and swear by the *Wild Soccer Bunch* logo. Do it for me. Do it in secret, under your blanket or hiding in a closet, but do it. I need your help. I need you to trust me. If you don't swear this oath, this story might take a terrible turn.

Okay, fine. Don't do it then.

You don't want to lose your place or buy something sight-unseen. I get it. I wouldn't want to either. Trust is a rare commodity these days; it's very scarce. Okay, so fine, wait to learn more before you swear that oath. But bookmark this page and remember the page number if you can! And when it's time, when without your trust I will meet my doom, then you need to go back and swear the oath. Do we have a deal?

I was watching my mother make our lunches. She knew exactly what Josh and I wanted, she didn't even have to ask. My little brother called her lunches "sandwich magic" or "surprise meatjellycheese and go-gurtwiches." I, too, admired my mother's amazing ability to always make just the right food, say just the right word, and do just the right thing. Warming my hands on my cocoa cup, I wondered why my father wasn't here admiring her with us.

Not that this was anything new. My father was the big family secret. I hardly knew anything about him. My mother would probably say I knew everything I needed to know: that he was a great guy, that my mother really loved him, but that they just couldn't stay together. But really, all I knew was one thing: he was not here. He had disappeared way before Josh was born. And I knew he wasn't dead.

That's why I had a big secret too. My mother, Josh, and my friends thought I was just out getting breakfast rolls at the bakery, when really I would detour to the Grim Woods and hit the bakery on the way home. I wasn't planning on letting anyone in on my secret, either. Not even after I was spooked by what happened today.

The Eighth Dimension

By the time I got to school I had forgotten all about my encounter in the Grim Woods, the Graffiti Towers, and Mickey the bulldozer. That's because at school, I was part of the best soccer team in the whole wide world.

"All is well!" my little brother Josh, and I, Julian Fort Knox, the all-in one defender, greeted our friends. They responded with the rest of our slogan: "As long as you're wild!"

School started two weeks ago and we were bursting with pride. After all, we were in the fourth grade now. Tyler, our number 10, was in fifth grade already, and Josh had finally made it to first grade. No more kindergarten for him; he was determined to live wild and dangerous like the rest of us.

Larry supported him. Larry is our coach, the best coach in the whole wide world. Every day after school we go to the soccer field and practice. But today was different: riding like the wind on our mountain bikes, when we arrived at the field, we slammed on the brakes, and stared up at the gate in utter surprise. Our world was about to change.

Actually, not all of us stopped. Roger didn't. Mouth wide open and eyes locked on what hung above the gate, Roger rode straight through the gate, clipped the ladder that was under it, and crashed into the wooden fence that surrounded our soccer field. Larry, who had been standing on the ladder, grabbed the top of the gate as the ladder crashed to the ground, and hung there like he was on the edge of a cliff. One by one, his fingers let go until he finally dropped to the dirt, throwing up a cloud of dust. Roger didn't see him fall and he didn't even notice the screwdriver Larry dropped, right on his head. BONK! Eyes wide open, his coke bottle glasses with giant eyes behind them, Roger just stared at the thing hanging above the entrance gate.

"Hello Roger, been riding long?!" Larry set the ladder back and climbed up as if he had been doing it all day, dragging his bum leg behind him. "Now that you're here, how about handing me the screwdriver?"

Roger had no idea what Larry was talking about. He scratched his head precisely where the screwdriver had hit him. "What screwdriver?

Then he noticed the tool lying in his lap. He picked it up, looked at it, then waved it at Larry. "*This* screwdriver?"

He tried to jump up, but his foot was stuck in Larry's toolbox. "Ahh! Help!" He struggled and pushed and pulled at the toolbox until he was catapulted out and crashed into the fence a second time. Without another word, Roger climbed up the ladder, screwdriver in hand, his face now redder than his hair.

The sign above the entrance was huge. It said, *Devil's Pit,* in bright orange letters.

"Wow!" Roger murmured. "That is wild!"

"Wild as a bag of cats," Zoe hissed. She had been one of us for about two weeks now. Although she was a girl, Zoe had our utmost respect.

"Sick!" I acknowledged. "The wildest soccer field ever!"

"Sure is!" Josh exclaimed. "Hail the great Hag-of-gnats!"

Zoe gave the kid a look and was about to say something but the others reassured her not to worry about it. Josh didn't know what we were talking about half the time.

Larry turned around and instead of the usual grin, he just glared at us. Our smiles disappeared immediately. Something was wrong, but what? Speechless, we watched Larry tighten the last screw, limp down the ladder, and march onto the soccer field. We followed behind him at a respectful distance and gathered in front of his kiosk.

Larry looked us up and down. His eyes hidden in the shadows of his red baseball cap, he glared at each and every one of us.

"Soccer field? Is that what you call it? That's a joke! What world do you live in?"

We swallowed hard. But honestly, we had no clue what we had done wrong. Nonetheless, Larry was so furious, he balled his fists.

"Soccer field? How dare you? Now listen carefully because I am not going to repeat myself. From now on, anyone who calls this stadium a 'soccer field' will be banned from it. Is that clear?"

We looked at each, puzzled. "Stadium?"

But he wasn't done. "I asked you a question! Is that

clear?" Still glaring at us, he waited for an answer. So we just nodded. "Good. Now I'll tell you!" he grumbled, but a tiny smile betrayed his real mood.

"Starting today, you'll be playing in a *real club league*. From this day forward, you're playing in Division 8, against teams from all over the state!

"Dimension 8!" Josh exclaimed. "That's huge!"

Everyone laughed.

"Division 8," I said. "Not dimension."

"Josh is right," Larry smiled. "Playing for a real league adds a new dimension to our game. The battle for the championship title begins next Saturday with your first game. And the first game of a club league championship sure doesn't take place on some run-of-the-mill soccer field. Championship games are played in a *stadium*."

Now Larry couldn't hide his smile any more. "Welcome to the *Devil's Pit* guys, the new stadium of the *Wild Soccer Bunch!*"

With that, Larry turned around, and threw the huge breaker bar on the old electrical box. After some moaning and creaking, sparks flew, something zapped and hissed and crackled, and one by one, six bright lights thumped on around the field.

"Incredible!" I shouted. I was amazed, to say the least.

"OMG! Real floodlights!!" Roger was excited.

"What did you think?" Kevin laughed. "Did you think this was a nursery playground? Far out, dude! This *is* the *Devil's Pit!*" Ever since the game against Mickey the bulldozer and his *Unbeatables,* Kevin had been our leader. "Welcome to the wildest stadium in Division 8!" Kevin said, grabbing one of the lemonades Larry handed out.

"To Larry!" Tyler shouted, lifting his bottle. Tyler was Kevin's brother and had just turned ten.

"Yes, to Larry, the *Devil's Pit,* and real floodlights!" Roger cheered. And Josh, my little brother, shouted as loud as he could: "To the wildest stadium in Dimension 8!" And everyone cheered.

Tattoos and Other Dreams

Naturally, we practiced late that night. After all, we had to baptize those floodlights. After practice, we all went home and straight to bed, and when our parents were finally convinced that we were fast asleep and left us alone for the night, we snuck out one-by-one and met at Camelot. That's what we call our tree house. Josh and I built it in our backyard. It's three floors high, and ever since the gunslinger, a.k.a. Diego's mom, challenged us to fight the *Furies,* it's been our headquarters.

As usual, when something important, exciting, or dangerous was on our agenda, we moved the old wooden keg to the center of the room. One by one, we would put our arms on it, and while Larry, who was always with us, told his stories about the great soccer heroes of the past, guys like Pele, Maradona, and Cruyff, and compared them to Messi, Ronaldo, and Wayne Rooney, Tyler would use a black Sharpie and draw a real-looking tattoo on our arms of the *Wild Guy* above a set of cross-bones. The logo fits right in with the *Devil's Pit* and our pirate treasure map player contracts. The logo also goes well with Larry's stories, you know, the ones that captivated us for hours? And it goes perfectly with our dreams.

We dream of our own league, of our victories as the best soccer team in the whole world, and of our life with the *Wild Soccer Bunch,* friends you can trust and depend on. Always.

"Hey Julian! You okay?" Zoe asked suddenly. She stood in the doorway and looked at me.

I looked up at her, surprised. Then I looked around the room and only Zoe, Tyler, and Kevin were still there.

Everyone else had left. I must have lost track of time. Did I fall asleep? Why was my face wet? I quickly wiped the tears away: "I'm great. I'm fine."

"Really? You sure?" Tyler asked, and Kevin just looked at me.

"Of course! Go home, guys!" I laughed. "Tomorrow is going to be a tough day. I'm warning you, I don't think Larry is going to be as nice as he was today. The championship is at stake."

Zoe smiled. "Exactly!"

"All is well!" I assured her.

"As long as you're wild," Tyler said and left with Zoe.

But Kevin stayed. He just looked at me.

"Julian, we are counting on you!" he said and looked into my eyes and into my soul.

I nodded.

I'd never let my friends down. Ever.

Beyond the Grim Woods
and Across the Prairie

I was still sure of my resolve to never let my friends down the next day. At school everything was business as usual. But at home, at 44 Dearborn Street, I had trouble even sitting still. After dinner I went straight to my room. Math homework took me forever, and when my little brother called from the kitchen, "Hey, where are you, Julian? Practice starts in exactly ten minutes!" I tore open my door and yelled at him, "Yes, and in one minute, it will start in *nine* minutes. Stop being such a pest! I'm not a kid anymore! I know how to get to the stadium."

Josh looked at our mother, irritated. She just shrugged. Then he looked at me again. "Is that so? In that case, how about you just get lost!"

With that, he grabbed his backpack, and stormed out the kitchen door and into our backyard where he grabbed his bike and furiously rode off. I went back to my room and pretended to look busy, just in case someone came in to check on me – someone like my mom, for instance. But basically all I did was sit there listening and counting to 100. Then I ran out of my room as fast as I could so my mother wouldn't notice that I wasn't wearing my soccer cleats and didn't take my backpack. Don't worry, I'll explain.

I ran and ran, taking streets and alleys where I wouldn't meet any of my friends. I didn't stop until I reached the ruins of the old house. I was totally out of breath, and with a racing heart I walked as calmly as I could through the gate and continued slowly. I didn't stop until I reached the other end of the Grim Woods.

The barren wasteland of the Prairie lay in front of me. The Graffiti Towers on the other side were so tall they seemed to touch the sky. I was hiding in the high weeds. No one had seen me; I could have turned around. But somehow that wasn't an option any more.

I had to find him. It's not every kid who gets to play in a soccer stadium called the *Devil's Pit,* especially a stadium with lights!

I had to tell him. Just like Kevin, Danny, Fabio, and Alex had surely told their fathers, I had to tell mine. That much I knew I had to do. I realized it the day before at Camelot while Tyler was painting the *Wild Guy* on my wrist. I was thinking about my dad. That's what brought tears to my eyes. I imagined how happy my father would be when I told him all about it, and when I invited him to a Division 8 championship game.

I took a deep breath. This was one of the hardest things I'd ever done. Then I marched on. Yesterday the weeds seemed to part for Mickey and his *Unbeatables.* Not for me. The tall brush hit my face, arms, and legs. I didn't care; I marched on until I finally reached the Prairie.

I looked around. Everything seemed desolate. Grass and thistles grew all around me on the dusty ground; and although it was broad daylight, a rat scurried past my feet.

I must have jumped a mile. I stopped. I prayed for a reason to turn around. But there was none. I had no doubt that my father was in there, somewhere. He had to be. It was a place on Earth like no other. Even my mom knew very little about it even though she knew more about every other place in the whole world than anyone. The news and the newscasters talked about remote places like Tasmania or Pago Pago. But they never mentioned anything about the Graffiti Towers behind the Grim Woods across the Prairie. Not ever.

So I marched on and crossed the Prairie and tried to ignore the rustling noises all around my feet. It couldn't be that hard to find him. All I had to do was find a nameplate that read *Michael Phillips*. I knew that once I found my father, he'd protect me.

I was sure of that and when I reached the parking lot near the Graffiti Towers, I was less afraid.

The wind howled and the grey concrete rose up like the pyramids of Egypt. The towers moaned and creaked like monsters about to awaken. The graffiti on the wall told stories of what would happen if they did. I stared at the new tattoo on my wrist to help me summon up enough courage to get through this, but compared to the images on the walls here, the *Wild Guy* looked like a sticker of a flower or an apple they give you in the dentists' office.

I was scared! But I warned you at the beginning of this story, didn't I? Better look for a safe place to hide, is what I said; best to stand with your back to the wall and always carry a flashlight. Well, I might have downplayed the risks. If so, I'm really sorry, but now it's too late.

Then again, maybe not. I was alone, after all. No Mickey or any other *Unbeatable* was in sight. I sucked in another breath and walked towards the first apartment building, fists clenched, ready for anything. The glass entrance door was cracked and looked like a spider web, and I prayed that the spider wasn't home. Then I started reading the nameplates.

"Phillips, Phillips, Phillips," I whispered, "Come on Phillips!" But the more I searched, the more my courage faded. No thank you, I wouldn't want to deliver the mail here. Most of the nameplates were rusty; some had been torn off. Some had dozens of different tags glued on top

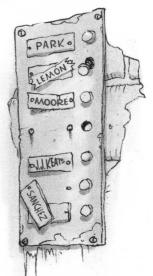

of each other. It was as if the people who lived here didn't really have names.

But I didn't give up. Mickey the bulldozer and his *Unbeatables* were nowhere in sight, so maybe this was my lucky day. And maybe there was a tenant by the name of Phillips in one of the other apartment buildings.

Slowly I walked through the parking lot toward the second tower. It seemed as if shadows were lurking all around me. But I just ignored them, like the rats on the Prairie. When I arrived, the door leading to the second apartment building slammed in my face. I stood there, motionless. I heard snickering, but I couldn't see anyone. I convinced myself that I had imagined it, and marched up the steps to the second apartment building.

Everything was different. The entrance door wasn't broken and the nameplates were all clean and easy to read.

"Phillips, Phillips, Phillips," I began to read, and "Phillips, Phillips, Phillips," echoed in my head.

That's when I smelled the stench, like a thick cloud enveloping me. "Yuck!" I thought and tried to catch a breath of fresh air. But my breath stammered and I rattled like an elephant seal coming up for air. Then I got it. The snickering. The echo. Neither of them were in my head!

The realization made me sweat. I prayed silently, "Please God, don't let it be true."

I turned around slowly and... I was staring straight into the beady eyes of Mickey the Bulldozer.

"Hello, loser!" he snarled. "Mickey the bulldozer from Mars. And I *don't* come in peace."

I looked at him as if he was speaking another language: Martian, maybe. Then I turned around quickly and tried to run. But the door behind me opened and Octopus, the Grim Reaper, and Kong blocked my way. I was trapped. Even though I couldn't see the other jerks, I knew they were out there somewhere in the parking lot, just waiting for me to try to escape.

There was no way out. I had to face the monster of all

monsters and not a single *Wild Bunch* friend was around to help me. I couldn't use the trick with Sox either, you know, like Diego did? Because never in his life would Sox be stupid enough to walk through the Grim Woods and across the Prairie to the Graffiti Towers. What was I thinking?!

With nothing left to lose, I slowly turned back to Mickey. He grinned like the bellhop at a zombie hotel.

I only had time for one thought: "Is this as friendly as he gets?"

That was it. I have no idea what happened after that.

A Pact with the Devil

When I started thinking clearly again, I was at the far
end of the parking lot between the Graffiti Towers. I lay
spread-eagled in the back of a pick-up truck and Mickey
the Bulldozer was leering down at me. Whatever was in
my pockets was strewn next to him and he was carefully
picking through the loot, his Darth Vader t-shirt barely
covering his huge belly.

"Leave my stuff alone!" I shouted at him. "It's all junk!" I hurried to say.

"Tell me something I *don't* know," Mickey grumbled, obviously disappointed. Then he noticed the foxtail. "Aha!"

He picked it up carefully and looked at it like a monkey looks at a banana. My fears dissipated momentarily. "Maybe he'll take a bite," I hoped briefly, "and then he'll grow hair on his tongue. Yuck!" But Mickey was smarter than a monkey – barely. He may not have been able to tell the difference between a foxtail and a squirrel. But he recognized the foxtail he thought was a squirrel.

"Check it out!" he yelled to his fellow gang members, wagging the tail. "Octopus, does this look familiar?"

Octopus startled awake from the slumber all *Unbeatables* fall victim to as soon as Mickey starts to think. Don't get me wrong, I had a lot of respect for them. Alligators slumber in the swamp until they suddenly SNAP! And just like an alligator, Octopus turned around and looked at his leader, fangs ready to chomp.

"The little twerp tricked us!" Mickey snarled. Then his beady eyes sparkled, and quick as lightning, as if the laws of gravity didn't apply, Mickey heaved his big body from the roof of the truck and stomped over to me.

"This little loser doesn't have anything we want. But worse, this little loser tried to trick us.

"What do you mean, *tried,*" I thought. Good thing I didn't say it out loud; I don't think they would have appreciated it.

"Yesterday, when we were coming back with our loot, he spied on us," Mickey said and the rest of his brutes sucked in breaths of surprise.

With that, Mickey the Bulldozer grabbed me with hands as big as hubcaps and lifted me up until I could no longer touch the ground. All of a sudden these guys looked so huge, they dwarfed me, and at that precise moment, I didn't feel wild anymore. Mickey took a deep breath and blew my checkered cap right off my head!

"We're done playing games, Sherlock. Got that?!" he hissed and threw me through the air.

I crashed into the truck cab and crumpled to the deck. The last bit of my confidence was crushed. It got real quiet, as quiet as my situation was serious. The other alligators around me began moving in. "Fight," was the word that would wake them up, and unlike Mickey, their muscles were not hampered by gobs of fat. The rattle of the bicycle chain the Grim Reaper took from his chest chilled me to the bone. I knew I was sitting on a time bomb ready to explode.

If only my little brother Josh would show up. He is like a superhero and always shows up at the last minute and saves the day. But when I thought about it, I knew better. He was where he was supposed to be: training with the *Wild Soccer Bunch* at the *Devil's Pit*.

Moaning and heaving, Mickey kneeled down in front of me, and his beady eyes stared into the deepest caverns of my soul.

"What are we going to do with you?" he wondered with fake compassion that made my blood curdle. "What ever shall we do?"

"Forget this ever happened?" I stammered. "I sure didn't mean any trouble, so why don't I just get up and leave you to your usual criminal activity."

I tried to get up and one of Mickey's hubcap hands darkened the sky and pinned me to the back of the truck.

"I said, what shall we do with you?" he was lost in thought, ignoring everything I said.

"Torture him?" Octopus suggested as if he was asking the others to play checkers.

"Good idea!" the Grim Reaper said.

"And dislocate his toes! So he won't be able to play any more with the *Wild Soccer Bunch!*"

Yikes. I swallowed hard. I liked my toes just the way they are!

Kong, the monumental creature from the Prairie of Mongolia, let his words melt on his tongue. Then he folded his hands and cracked his fingers and my toes curled up inside my shoes like ten little turtles. It didn't help. I couldn't escape. I was like dough trapped in a waffle iron. A waffle iron being held down by a bulldozer. I couldn't move, even if I wanted to. "Okay, so torture first, then the dislocation of the toes," I said, trying to stall them, getting ready to accept my fate. If I was lucky, I would pass out during the torture phase. Wait a sec. I was Julian Fort Knox, the all-in-one defender, and the boys surrounding me were complete morons. Pulling my tail between my legs and giving up would be like Real Madrid losing to the *Tiny Town Cuties*.

"Hang on a minute!" I said with determination. "Let's think this through. Maybe there's a better way. Maybe I can be of use to you," I said with calm desperation.

I looked at them with promise in my eyes. It wasn't easy, because I didn't have a clue what I was trying to sell these bullies, I just wanted to survive!

Octopus, Grim Reaper, and Kong seemed to think the same. They looked as if someone had just stolen their dessert. That's how much torturing me meant to them.

"Well, well, well!" Mickey hissed. "As a matter of fact, there is something you can do for us."

"Uh-oh," I thought. On the one hand, I felt so happy that moment I almost believed it was Christmas. On the other hand, happiness usually doesn't last, and this was no exception.

"Money!" he murmured. "Money is scarce around here. I think you know what I mean?"

I looked at the ugly Graffiti Towers and knew *exactly* what he was talking about.

"But on Chicago's North Side," he continued, "where you come from, there's plenty of dough."

Kyle's mansion on posh Woodlawn Avenue immediately came to mind. And Fabio's castle on 13 Heaven's Gate. Holy McMansion! What had I done?

Mickey didn't share my horror.

"When parents are rich, kids usually get a big allowance. Am I right or am I right? What if we just make sure that money gets redistributed this way? How about we detour your friends' allowance from their pockets to ours? You think you can handle that for us?"

He looked at me expectantly and I swear I was trying everything to show my disgust. I wanted to refuse vehemently, or at least shake my head 'no'. But my toes, well, I liked them totally located and when they wiggled, they were more persuasive than me.

Mickey smiled happily, triumphantly. He knew he had won the day.

"Okay. Deal. Payday is tomorrow night. Don't be late."

He finally let go of me. I didn't hesitate for an instant and jumped up and started shoveling my stuff back into my pockets. A shadow engulfed me. I stopped dead in my tracks.

The owner of the pick-up truck stood right in front of me.

"What are you doing here?" he asked.

I looked around. The *Unbeatables* were gone; vanished into the night.

"What are you doing here?" the driver asked again. "I've never seen you around here." Then his expression softened. "Are you alright? Do you need help?"

I let out a sigh of relief and my life stopped flashing in front of my eyes. The truck driver wasn't going to finish the job started by Mickey and the *Unbeatables* –

he wanted to help me! I couldn't speak. I couldn't think of a thing to say. But my feet knew what to do. I ran.

Big mistake. When I charged onto the Prairie, Mickey was there waiting for me.

"Hold it right there, twerp!" he yelled, and I did. "Tomorrow night! Payday! Don't forget. If you don't hold up your end of the bargain, I'll send the Grim

Reaper and Kong and Octopus to show you the error of your ways."

I nodded, dumbly, I'm sure, I was so scared.

"Good night then," Mickey said politely. "See you at school."

Manners were the last thing on my mind. I ran as fast as I could. And for the first time in my life, I wished I were Danny, the world's fastest midfielder.

Where Have You Been, Julian?

When I got home, the first thing I did was hug everyone. Needless to say, they weren't expecting it.

"I'm back," I shouted happily. "Back in the home I love; back with the people I love! Home sweet home!"

I gave my mom another hug as she was leaving the kitchen.

My brother Josh looked at me funny. So I planted a big wet kiss on his forehead. And he socked me in the stomach. "Ew!" he shouted, backing away. "Get away from me!"

But I was so grateful I was alive, I just beamed at my brother like he was an angel. I stuck out my chin. "Put one there if you want, bro," I said and he didn't hesitate a nanosecond to hit me a good one. And I went down. For a few seconds, I didn't know where I was. Then I looked up at my brother and there were two of him!

"Holy guacamole!" I shouted. "That's what I call brotherly love!"

"Are you nuts?!" he said, moving even further away from me.

I rubbed my sore chin and grinned at him: "Maybe."

That's when Josh looked at his fist, at me, and realized what he'd done. "I'm crazier than you! What's *wrong* with you?"

"Just glad to see you, bro," I said.

He must have been embarrassed because he let out a big sigh and stared at his feet.

That's when my mom came back in the kitchen. "You're both crazy, if you ask me."

"Julian's lost it, Mom," Josh announced, then marched out of the kitchen.

"Maybe," I yelled after him. "But can't I be happy to see you and Mom without getting punched in the stomach and socked in the jaw?"

My mother sat at the kitchen table and put garlic into the garlic press. She looked at me carefully and then smashed with all her might.

"Where were you, Julian?" she asked and all I wanted to do was hug her again. I wanted to tell her the truth. I wanted to tell her I was in hell, but I didn't. If she knew how rough it was out there with those bullies, she might not let me play anymore. No, keeping quiet was the best approach in this situation and that's how we left it.

"Out," I said.

Same thing happened the next day at school.

"Come on, Julian, tell me, where were you yesterday?" Roger called out to me. "*Dimension 8* is really tough," he said. After the other day, no one called it *Division 8* again. As far as the *Wild Soccer Bunch* was concerned, it was *Dimension 8,* because we were so happy it felt like we had all been transported to the 8th Dimension.

"Everyone else in our division is a year older and most of them are bigger than us," Roger continued. "Larry had to sign us up in that division so Tyler could play. We need you, man. Without you, our defense is Swiss cheese."

The other members of the *Wild Soccer Bunch* looked at me long and hard. But that wasn't all. I could feel enemy eyes on me, too, and they burnt like charcoal in a barbecue. Honest, the ground beneath my feet turned hot and it felt as if I was dancing barefoot on hot coals.

I felt rotten inside, and I know Mickey the bulldozer loved every minute of it. There he was in all his grossness, standing at the edge of the schoolyard, under the trees, leering at me.

"Hey! You all right?" Zoe asked. It must have shown in my face, but I quickly hid it again. I was humiliated, but I couldn't tell *her* that.

"I'm fine," was all I said.

"Really? Well, tell that to your face!" Tyler said.

But Kevin saw right through me. There was no "Julian, we're counting on you!" No "All is well as long as you're wild!" He just looked at me, and I knew he didn't believe a word I said.

Man! I was too young to be stressed out. I wanted to tell them what happened. I wasn't a liar and I sure wasn't a traitor. I was part of the *Wild Soccer Bunch*. My friends would protect me. Mickey the Bulldozer could kiss my goal post. That was it; I'd had it. I would tell Kevin and Tyler and Zoe what happened. Yeah, that's what I was going to do – tell the truth.

But then I heard a bubble pop. Someone was chewing gum. Mickey. I turned around and there was Octopus, Grim Reaper, and Kong. Like tiger sharks in a kiddy pool, coming right at me. I was about to be in the middle of a feeding frenzy.

Too Good to Be True

I got out of there as fast as I could and later, I had trouble concentrating in class and I was really nervous when Danny called a meeting at the break.

"Larry's birthday is coming up. Next Saturday, the day of our first game in *Dimension 8,*" he said. "I think we should all bring our allowance to the *Devil's Pit* today. Larry really needs a suit."

We didn't get it. "A dress suit?" Josh asked.

"Come on!" Danny moaned. "Don't you guys know anything about soccer? We have this great uniform with our logo and these bright orange socks. But Larry always shows up in his ratty old street clothes. They're so ragged you can't tell his pants from his shirt and his socks are so dirty they stand up by themselves! The coaches of real teams are dressed to kill, and that's why we should give Larry a suit for his birthday. A sharp suit with a tie with the team colors on it."

The other kids on the team loved the idea of getting Larry a new suit of clothes. But I kept hearing Mickey's voice telling me what he was going to do to me if I didn't deliver the allowances of all the team members. I couldn't do that to my friends, especially since we needed to buy Larry a suit. What was I going to do? And just when I thought there was no way out of this mess, I got an idea.

This time, it was me who hurried Josh to practice. Like a tiger in a cage, I paced our kitchen floor at 44 Dearborn Street. Finally, we took our bikes and raced to the *Devil's Pit*.

We practiced better than we ever had before. Our plan was to counter attack. That's how Larry wanted to beat the older teams. Kyle, the Invincible, would charge out of his goal and kick the ball way past the halfway line. That's where Alex the cannon Alexander, Tyler, our number 10, Zoe the fearless, or I, Julian Fort Knox, would control it and pass it to the wings. Our wingers would head close to the touchlines and our forwards would make

the run into the penalty area. Danny, our fastest player, would thunder the ball into the net like a torpedo, or pass it to Kevin, the star striker, who would sink the ball into the goal. We also had more options to our attack: Diego, the tornado, or Joey, would come from the right or the left so Fabio, the wizard, would close the deal with a magic play: a bicycle kick into the goal or a double pass with Tyler, that would most definitely bring any goalkeeper to tears.

We felt like the best team in the world, and even Larry, who would usually ask more and more of us, sat down on the grass and just watched. That's how happy he was with our performance.

But I was the happiest of them all. I was one of the *Wild Soccer Bunch* again and when Danny collected our allowance for Larry's present, I was sure I would never betray my friends. Never ever.

It's time to swear the oath now. Go on, go back to the page you bookmarked earlier, and if you didn't already do it, do it now. I know you're skeptical and I deserve it, but I will prove my loyalty to you. Ready?

Our allowance wasn't nearly enough to buy a suit for Larry. We were real disappointed for a while. But then I had an idea. We'd collect more money tomorrow. Everyone was supposed to ask parents, uncles, grandmas, grandpas, and aunts for a donation towards the present for Larry.

"What do you say?" I asked proudly.

The others looked at me surprised, particularly Tyler, Zoe, and Kevin.

Then Zoe smiled. "All is well!" she said.

"As long as you're wild!" I responded with a laugh, and Tyler lifted his hand for a high five with me. We formed our usual circle, put our arms around each other's shoulders, and as Kevin looked deep into my eyes, we counted to three and screamed at the top of our lungs: "1-2-3-WILD!"

Our battle cry was loud enough to be heard through the Grim Woods and across the Prairie, all the way to the Graffiti Towers. That gave me the courage to do what I had to do and go where I had to go: through the Grim Woods, across the Prairie to the Graffiti Towers.

To Hell and Back

At home at 44 Dearborn I was really quiet and pretended to be tired. No one was ready for this because I'm never quiet and I'm never tired. Then, when I didn't bother watching my half-hour of TV before bed, Josh couldn't take it any more.

"Mom, I'm telling you, Julian has lost it!" he said as he got up from the kitchen table and turned on TV.

Usually I would have clipped him for such a remark, but this time I just yawned and stretched, then watched the last few seconds of a Champions League game, my favorite tournament. I'd never missed a single game, by the way. Then I forced a barely audible "nighty-night," got up as if I was at least a hundred years old, and slouched off to my room.

I went to bed fully dressed. Luckily, I noticed that my pajamas were still on the chair, jumped out of bed, grabbed them, and stuffed them in bed next to me just before my mom appeared at the door.

"Phew!" I thought and pulled the blanket all the way up to my throat.

My mom looked at me with suspicion, but not overly concerned. She was about to leave, but then her worries about me won out.

"Can I trust you?" she asked and I said, "Of course," and she said, "No, can I trust you to come to me when you need help?" I swallowed the huge lump in my throat.

"Sure," I answered, less sure than I'd ever been about anything. At least I wasn't lying. My plan was good and I'd make everything right that night.

"Okay, honey. Good night!" my mom finally said and I knew she believed me. "Sleep well!"

I waited until she tucked Josh into bed – and sat down at the grand piano. I love falling asleep to her playing. But that night I got up, took my piggy bank off the shelf, and climbed out the window into the night.

Out in the street, I wrapped my piggy bank in my jacket, grabbed a stone and hit it. It made almost no noise and neither Josh nor my mother could possibly have heard anything. I picked the $42.24 from the shards, stuffed the money into my pockets, poured the shards into the bushes, and was about to run off, when I stopped dead in my tracks.

In the house across the street, Danny stood at the window of his room and looked directly at me. I jumped behind the bushes and prayed that he couldn't see me. Then I realized that you can't see out if you turn on the light at night. Relieved, I came out of hiding and ran off. I ran and ran and never noticed that Danny's eyes followed me all the way. His window was open, and he saw me clear as day. But I didn't know that. I ran and ran and didn't stop until I reached at the other end of the Grim Woods.

The dark Prairie stretched out before me. I came here often. The last time, just before dawn, was when I'd come to the old house ruins to toss my coin. I dropped to the ground then and spread my arms between my world and the other and tried to see which side pulled my heart more. One thing I never liked doing was crossing the Prairie at night. I'd done it before, but I didn't like it.

The tall weeds hit my legs, and I couldn't help thinking about the rats that reigned there in the terrain, day or night. I knew it would be worse at night because more of them would be out.

I marched on nonetheless. Thistles clawed at my ankles. Shards of glass crunched under my shoes, and glowing, beady eyes peered out at me from the darkness. The furry things scurried past my feet, chased by naked pink tails. Suddenly the ground around me seemed to swarm with rats.

That was enough to send me running. Maybe I had been running all along; I can't remember. Even in broad daylight this place scared me, nothing was worse than the fear that made my heart race that night. The Graffiti Towers loomed menacingly in the blackened sky, and the cars cowered in their presence as if they were the larger, fatter brothers of the rats I had just fled. To keep the fear away, I made up a name for them: R.O.E.S. *Rats of Enormous Size.*

Man! What was I doing here!? Why didn't I just curse Mickey the bulldozer and run off? Not a bad idea, but ideas are easy. Making them work is hard. How do you curse Mickey the bulldozer when he is right in front of you? His flashlight was pointed right at me and blinded me. Truth be told, I was blind with fear when I recognized the shadows of the flies swirling around that monster Mickey: Humongous, Mow-down, Juggernaut, Octopus, Grim Reaper, and Kong.

"Boohoofrickedydoo!" Mickey murmured. "The dwarf had the guts to show up. I think he deserves a medal!"

Mickey held his enormous belly as he laughed. I could feel the steam rising inside me. Those morons had tricked me. They never expected me to show up. All my worries, my guilty conscience, my fears, the sense of gloom and impending doom I had felt all day and all night – even my declaration of love for Josh – well, I worried about it for nothing. You know what? I never seem to worry about the things that are happening, only about the things that are about to happen. And what I worried about was as unnecessary as a wart – a wart that grew and grew until it was as big as Mickey's big fat face.

"Well, since you're here, show me what you got!" He grabbed me, whirled me 180 degrees and up into the air, and held me by my feet until all of my $42.24 fell out of my pockets.

Plink plink plink! The money from my shattered piggy bank scattered into the dirt. "Hey! What do you know? A real treasure!" Mickey was amazed and he dropped me like a sack of potatoes.

"Octopus! Grab the loot!" he barked. He didn't talk to me, of course; in fact, he didn't even look at me. I had ceased to exist, and you won't believe how happy that made me. I had done it. I had averted danger. I wouldn't have to betray my friends. I had given these nitwits enough money to satisfy their sickening greed.

"Let's go! Move it!" Mickey ordered. "My cousin bought a grocery truck full of goodies yesterday, if you

know what I mean."

I didn't know what he meant and I didn't care. But I would soon.

The others jeered, and while Octopus waved my money around as if it was my scalp, they marched off. I was totally relieved and even thought for a moment that the Graffiti Towers were a safe place after all.

But then Mickey turned around.

"I almost forgot about you! Sorry about that, good buddy!" he purred. "And just so's we're clear: I expect another payment by Friday. Three times as much! Got that?"

"W-what? Are you nuts? Where am I supposed to get that kind of money?" I was appalled. "Forget it. There's no way I can do it."

"Really? I can't tell you how disappointed I am to hear that!" Mickey smiled. "And what about the money for Larry's birthday present? You're the one collecting it, ain't you?"

I was shocked. "How did you know about that?"

Mickey grinned, ear-to-ear. "I didn't. But now I do. In case you haven't noticed, we know a lot about you guys. Thanks for filling in the blanks."

I felt like a total idiot. I'd just fallen straight into their web.

Suddenly Mickey grabbed my hand and pulled me up.

"See? There's a solution for everything!" he winked at me. "And I have total faith that a guy like you can figure it out."

He squeezed my hand so hard it cracked. I winced in pain. But Mickey didn't seem to notice or care. He leaned into me:

"I like you, wild dwarf. We can go places together. As long as you do what I tell you."

He squeezed even harder. This time, I whimpered. "As long as you know who's boss," he added, narrowing his eyes. "And no tricks!"

He was about to smash my hand. I screamed in pain, and finally he had mercy on me and let go.

"That's what I like to hear," he smiled. "Take care, moneybags. See you Friday. Oh! And enjoy the rest of your evening!"

He waved at me, and for a minute he looked like Humpty Dumpty. A mean, disgusting, uncrackable Humpty Dumpty. Then he marched away and caught up with the rest of his merry band of bullies.

I waited until the night swallowed him up, then I just stood there, motionless. I wanted to be absolutely sure he wasn't coming back. I didn't want to ever see him again.

I looked at my poor hand. It hurt, but it was okay, but when I turned it over to inspect it, my eyes fell on the *Wild Soccer Bunch* tattoo. Some friend I was. Tomorrow was Thursday. Tomorrow would be my last day as a member of the *Wild Soccer Bunch*.

Suddenly I couldn't contain my anger anymore and I screamed. I screamed as loud as I could.

"Father! Can you hear me? Father! This is Julian! Julian Fort Knox, the all-in-one defender. I swear, Father, I will never betray my friends. Never ever, you hear!"

Then I wiped the tears off my face and added softly: "Not if I can help it, anyway."

Suddenly a light came on a few feet ahead of me. It was the reading light in the pick-up truck and it lit up the driver's face. It was the man from the night before. My guardian angel. He had a kind face and I imagined he was ready to help me, that he'd always have my back. I snapped out of it. He must have been watching the whole time. I wanted to stay, but I couldn't. I couldn't help it. So I ran away.

No Safer Place on Earth

For some reason, I felt great the next morning. When I woke up, the sun was shining into my room, its golden rays freeing the idea that would save my life.

Mickey the bulldozer and his friends had not expected that I'd show up the first time. So why would they this time? All I had to do was forget about what had happened the night before; you know, the way you forget about a nightmare? Then everything would go back to normal. There's nothing easier than forgetting a dream once you're awake.

When I came down to breakfast, Josh covered his face, because he was sure I'd kiss him again. But I only kissed my mom. I kissed her to make up for the worry I had caused her. I was proud of myself; I had kept my promise. My problems were solved and nobody noticed a thing.

School flew by that day and one of the reasons was that Mickey didn't show up. No doubt he and his gang had used my money to buy a ton of stolen candy from his cousin, and more than likely they were baking in the sun somewhere, stomachs fat and full of that candy. But I didn't care. I didn't care about the money, either. In my mind, it wasn't a bad investment; any time spent without Mickey was worth twice what I paid for it. I was in such a good mood that I even convinced myself that Danny had forgotten about what he had seen last night – when I broke my piggy bank in the street right in front of his window.

Or was he just acting? Did the *Wild Soccer Bunch* know about my meeting with Mickey? It seemed like it sometimes. The way they looked at me when they thought I didn't notice. Those glances spoke volumes.

Forget it! No way! This was nothing but plain old paranoia. What was I worried about? I didn't have anything to hide! I didn't do anything wrong! Mickey and his thugs were terrorizing me and I was starting to lose my mind!

After school we went to practice in the *Devil's Pit*. Although, when Larry benched me, I couldn't help thinking that even my own coach was suspicious of me. There it was again. That stinking paranoia. Larry had Sox and I play defense. We were supposed to put a monkey-wrench into the counter-attack of the other side and force them into a direct game play.

But Larry's plan didn't work. The *Wild Soccer Bunch,* especially Tyler, Fabio, Zoe, and Kevin were just too good. They outplayed us badly. We didn't have a chance. And when Kevin passed a ball between my legs like I was a total beginner, I threw in the towel. I totally gave up. Or rather, that's what I wanted to do, but then Sox stood in front of me, snarled back his lips, hid his bat ears behind his dinosaur teeth, and growled at me.

"Leave me alone. You don't understand what's happening to me! You're just a dog!" I hissed and marched off the field.

I hadn't even taken three steps when I heard a whimper. I turned around, and there was that wacky dog again, running after me. He shoved his tail between his legs and whined and whimpered, louder and louder. I swear, he looked like he had a grin on his face. Honest. You may not believe this, but Sox is smart enough to plaster a grin on his face and this was just too much for me. Sox was mocking me! Give me a break! No dog was allowed to do that! I wasn't running off with my tail between my legs – was I?

I balled my fists and stood my ground. "Fine!" I hissed, relenting. "You win. Let's show them."

And show them we did. The others didn't have a

chance. I was the angriest all-in-one defender ever.
I played better than even the most stubborn ankle-biting terrier ever could, so Sox saw no reason to keep playing. Satisfied he had done his duty, he sat on the sidelines watching, barking and howling his applause, and when I fell to the ground, exhausted after my last and best goal-saving slide, he ran over to me and licked my face. The *Wild Soccer Bunch* came running, too, and congratulated me. Larry even carried me on his shoulders to the kiosk. There he handed out lemonade and old soccer stories. We hung around until it got dark, and when Larry left, Danny collected the money for his birthday present.

"$221," he counted the bills and coins. "That should do it. We can't buy him a nice new Armani suit with it, but there's this second-hand shop my mother goes to all

the time. They have some good deals there. Think about it. Larry in a suit. We won't recognize him!"

Danny smiled at us, and based on his grin we all imagined just what kind of suit he was talking about. Then he grabbed my cap and poured in the money.

"Here you go, Julian!" He gave the cap back to me. "You're in charge of our money."

Uh-oh, I thought. "Me?" I was flabbergasted.

"Yes, you!" Danny answered and looked me in the eye. "Your name is Fort Knox, isn't it? There's no safer place for money on earth than Fort Knox! Right?" he asked looking around at the other members.

Danny and I looked around at the same time, but none of the *Wild Soccer Bunch* disagreed. I blushed and whispered a hoarse, "Thanks!" Then I took my cap and shoved it with the money into my pocket.

"Great!" Danny smiled. "Then all's well!"

"As long as you're wild!" I responded weakly, but then I took my bike and rode home, and the closer I got, the more I was bursting with pride. They trusted me. They really did.

When I took a shower, I left the curtain open so I could keep an eye on my pants with the money in it, even though the soap and shampoo burned in my eyes. Then I stuck my pants under my pillow for safe keeping.

I thought about my father again. If only he knew how much my friends trusted me. He would be so happy. Then I fell asleep.

The Sea Monster Kraken
Feel-Good Dream

I slept soundly and calmly and at some point I dreamed
I was in the ocean. I dove through the waves like a fish,
when suddenly something touched my toes. Scared, I
looked into the depths. Seven fat and milky jellyfish
floated around me. One of them had a Mohawk. They
all had the faces of the *Unbeatables*. Fat, wobbly, and
indistinguishable from the goopy, wiggly, jellyfish,
they tried to catch me with their sticky tentacles. They
pushed and pulled at what I was carrying in my arms.
Then I realized what I was carrying! It was the cap with
the money in it for Larry's birthday present.

"No! You can't have it!" I wanted to scream, but
you can't scream under water. You can only make this
low muffled noise that sounds like a roar. And that's
precisely what Mickey-the-bulldozer jellyfish did. He
roared loudly as he swam directly towards me and all I
could do was swim away in desperation. I shot to the
surface like an arrow, flew into the sky, and bumped into

something big and red.

"Oops! Sorry! I didn't see you coming!" said the boy with red curls and coke-bottle glasses as he flew around me. "Hey Julian, where have you been?"

"Roger? Is that really you?" I was shocked. "I didn't know you could fly."

"What do you mean? You can too. It's great, isn't it?" he answered and somersaulted in front of me.

That's when I realized that I was flying too. I looked down at the ocean fifty yards below. Wow! It was amazing. I spread my arms, performed a flawless loop, and then swooped down, lying on my back, and shot across the water just above the waves.

That's when I heard a whoosh. Right next to me, a fountain of water shot up like a blue tornado. Whoosh! Whoosh! Whoosh! Seven explosions went off, and seven jellyfish jumped up.

"Roger! Watch out!" I yelled. "It's the *Unbeatables*. These jerks want the money!"

But Roger remained calm. He just sat there, cross-legged as if on an invisible flying carpet. He was super cool.

"Finally! About time!" he said.

"What? Are you nuts? Those are monster kraken." I yelled at him. "We have to get out of here!"

But Roger just laughed at me.

"There aren't any monsters! It's not even Halloween!"

Roger was nuts! There were seven *Unbeatables*, and Roger and I didn't stand a chance against them. They'd gobble us up and their wobbly stomachs would digest us in the blink of an eye.

"Come on! Let's go!" I yelled.

But instead, Roger pulled a needle from his pocket

and handed it to me. "If they are sea monsters, then I'm not really flying." He took a second needle from his pocket and attacked.

"They're just balloons, Julian!" he yelled and popped one. "You see? What did I tell you! Dumb, fat, balloons!" He popped the second.

The balloon with the Mohawk appeared right in front of me and with quick reflexes I poked it in the nose. Pop! I finally got it. Pop pop! Grim Reaper and Kong were obliterated! Roger took care of Juggernaut and in the end we both grabbed the string of Mickey's balloon and loosened it: "PHHHHHT!" the fat balloon crisscrossed through the air, "PHHHHHT!" until it was nothing but a wrinkly, rubber rag and sunk into the foamy water below.

"This is the best dream of my life!" I thought, still sleeping. Then, still dreaming, I stretched, yawned and looked forward to the morning.

Fort Knox

I slept like a baby and didn't wake up until the sun
tickled my nose. I blinked. In no time I jumped out of
bed, grabbed my pants from underneath my pillow, and
put them on.

I was looking forward to seeing my friends and to
the training in the afternoon. And, of course, to buying
Larry's birthday present. We'd buy it with the money I
had guarded all night. It was still in my cap, which was
in my pants.

My mom sniffed disapprovingly when I walked into
the kitchen. "When was the last time you changed your
pants? You're not wearing those to school again, are you?"

I looked down. She was right. My pants weren't
exactly fresh. I had probably worn them for seven days
by now and to tell you the truth – they stank.

"Well?" my mom nagged. "Will you please be so kind
as to wear something a little less – gross?"

"No, I can't!" I refused, calmly taking my seat at the
table.

"Julian, please!" my mother ordered. I love it that even when she's angry she's polite.

"Julian, there are five – I repeat, five – clean pairs of pants in your closet."

"I know that," I said and took a roll from the bowl on the table. "And I know that these are slightly gross. But there are more important things in life than what scent I am giving off at any given time."

With that bit of intellectual wisdom, I put butter and jelly on my roll and took a hungry bite. My mother just kept staring at me, the wrinkles on her face deepening with every tick of the clock.

"Yes," I said. "That's how it is. I am Julian Fort Knox the all-in-one defender and these pants are my bank vault."

My mother cocked her head to the side and looked at my little brother.

"It's true, mom," Josh confirmed seriously. "Fort Sox is the safest place on earth."

"You see? What did I tell you?!" I grinned. "You wouldn't want to be responsible for Mickey and his gang stealing Larry's birthday money, would you?"

I stopped myself and winced. If I could have stuffed those words back in my mouth I would have done it in a heartbeat. What had I just said? Nobody knew about

Mickey and me. Or did they? Josh and my mother just stared at me in surprise.

What were they thinking? Did they know? I had to get away. Immediately! Pronto!

"Well, okay then," I said, and wiped my mouth with my hand. "I'll see you tonight. Training starts right after school. And then we're going to buy Larry a birthday present!" I stammered. Then I grabbed my backpack and ran out the back door, hopped on my bike, and pedaled away as if my life depended on it. It did.

My mother and Josh watched me ride furiously away with matching furrowed brows. Must be a family trait. At least, that's how I pictured them. It wasn't even a quarter after seven yet. School didn't start until eight and it was a short seven-minute ride to school. And I could almost hear their minds racing: "Why is Julian so afraid of Mickey and the *Unbeatables?*"

All for One

I pedaled as fast as I could. Only one more day, I
thought. Then this horrible nightmare would be over.
The money would be spent. And then – ha! – Mickey
could kiss my rosy red fire engine. Don't blame me for
saying that, I learned it from Larry. Speaking of Larry
– Larry would have the suit he so richly deserved. And
dressed in this suit he would be coaching us at 10 a.m.
on Saturday and leading us to our very first victory in
our first game in the *Devil's Pit*.

Oh man, in my head, the world was perfect and
everything felt great. I imagined it in bright colors. How
we'd put on our black jerseys with the *Wild Soccer Bunch*
logo on the chest; how we'd run out onto the field
wearing our bright orange shin guards; how we'd form
our circle. We'd stand arm in arm, screaming our battle
cry to the heavens.

"1-2-3-WILD!" Our voices would echo throughout the
town. It would be a great day. Yes, I was absolutely
certain that this is how it would go down.

I slowed down a bit and held my head into the wind. It was a little chilly and smelled like fall. It was probably one of the last days of summer, but I only noticed that when I saw Octopus in the street.

"Hey, Julian!" his voice cut through the air. "Having a nice day?"

I slumped and couldn't move any more. All I saw was his Mohawk and his lying eyes. What I didn't see was the red light when I was crossing the street.

"Julian! Watch out!" another voice yelled and I slammed on the brakes at the very last moment. A car sped through the intersection and almost hit me.

"Whoa, dude! That was close!" Roger yelled and stopped his bike right next to me. Filled with fear, his eyes stared at me from behind his coke bottle glasses.

"What's the matter with you?" he asked reproachfully, but I was watching Octopus who was sauntering over to us.

"Nothing!" I answered irritably. "I was just daydreaming."

"What's up with him?" Roger asked, meaning Octopus. "Is he a daydreamer too?" Roger just wouldn't let go.

"How should I know?" I lied and took off, although the light was still red. I didn't care. Roger took one more look at Octopus who came dangerously close. Then he shouted: "Hey Julian, wait for me!" and he took off after me.

The schoolyard was still deserted. Not even the teachers had arrived. When Roger and I locked our bikes, a cold wind blew into our faces. It was an icy wind from the darkest corners of the earth. And with this wind at their backs, Mickey and his gang flew towards us.

Roger took a few steps back.

"Okay, why are they coming this way? Are you going to tell me they don't want anything from you either?" he asked sarcastically.

"How should I know? I thought they were after you," I lied again and prayed that there was a superhero that would appear out of nowhere, right then and there.

But all my superheroes were around the whole time. I just didn't know it. They were all lying flat on the roof of the bike rack, just behind me, looking down on us. Kevin, Danny, Tyler, and Zoe and the rest of the *Wild Soccer Bunch* – everyone was there to help Roger and me – Diego the tornado, Fabio the wizard, and Alex the cannon Alexander. I heard later that they all flexed their muscles, ready to attack. But Kevin lifted his hand.

"No, not yet!" he whispered.

"Okay then, when?" Danny protested. "Only a few more steps and Mickey mows them down."

"I know!" Kevin said. "But this isn't a soccer game. We don't stand a chance!"

"I don't care!" Danny contradicted. "Those are our friends down there!"

"Mine too!" Zoe hissed. "We go on three!"

"No, we don't!" Kevin ordered. "Unless you want something bad to happen to Julian and Roger."

Zoe glared at him. Oh boy, if looks could kill. Fabio told me the way Zoe looked at Kevin scared even him. "This was your plan!" she said. "They are down there because of you!"

"Exactly, and that's why I'll get them out."

But he didn't. Not yet. Mickey approached us. He

towered over me like a tsunami. My right hand was reaching for the cap in my pocket. That's where the money was. The money they probably knew was there. Then Darth Vader stopped about two feet away from us and waited for his gang to assemble around him.

"Look what the rats dragged in," Roger finally said. Oh how I wish he hadn't said that.

Above them, the *Wild Soccer Bunch* didn't flinch. They stayed flat and silent on the roof and waited for a signal from Kevin.

"No, not yet!" he whispered and pointed towards the parking lot where the principal of our school, Mr. Carlson, had just parked. "We jump when he leaves the lot." Unfortunately, Mr. Carlson wasn't doing things in our time. In fact, he took his own sweet time. He carefully closed his car door. He straightened his tie. He put his hand to his mouth and smelled his own breath.

The *Wild Soccer Bunch* waited for what felt like an eternity.

Finally, the principal walked out of the parking lot.

"Now!" Kevin shouted.

With blood-curdling screams, the *Wild Soccer Bunch* leaped from the rooftop like a waterfall of black ninjas, grabbed the hands of the *Unbeatables,* and shook them like they were greeting them for the first time. Roger

and I were in shock!

"Hey, Octopus, long time no see!" Diego seemed overjoyed. "Where did you get that great tattoo? Or did the spider webs in your brain get scared and crawl out of your ears and onto your forehead?"

"Mickey!" Tyler yelled with his sweetest smile. "How many times do I have to flush before you go away?"

"And Grim-baby, you are still as dumb as a doorknob!" Zoe sung into the Grim Reaper's ear.

The *Unbeatables* were completely overwhelmed, but Roger and I were overjoyed. A minute ago they were convinced that Roger and I were easy prey. But then the black ninjas from the sky had fallen into their midst!

Suddenly, Mr. Carlson stood in front of us. He must have heard the commotion and come back. Grey and strict, he riveted us with disapproval over the rim of his frameless glasses. The Grim Reaper barely had enough time to hide his chain down the back of Octopus' pants.

Silence fell over us all like a blanket of snow.

Only the wind howled. And the wheels in Mickey's brain turned, trying to understand what had just happened. A fight was out of the question now. Not in front of the principal. Kevin's plan had worked perfectly. Roger and I were safe, and Mickey the bulldozer had no choice but to thank us for the friendly gesture. He grabbed my hand and squeezed it, hard enough to make me cry.

"No worries, we'll meet again, loser!" he whispered in my ear. "And a good morning to you, Mr. Carlson!" he said loudly.

He grinned as wide as he could, turned around, and stormed off. The other *Unbeatables* followed him like flies on an unguarded donut.

We wanted to celebrate our triumph, but the principal was still there, fiddling with his glasses, no doubt searching his brain for the right question. "What is the meaning of this, Roger? And Julian Phillips, what business do you have with Mickey?" That's when Josh, our official superhero, stepped up. He had come straight from home and as soon as he arrived, he picked up Mr. Carlson's briefcase.

"I'll carry this for you, sir," he smiled. "I love carrying briefcases, you know! I think James Bond had one just like this. Very impressive!" he said reassuringly, marching off. It took a second for the principal to pick up on what was happening, then realizing he had no choice, he started to chase after his briefcase, which was already halfway across the lot.

I was joyful! But Roger was furious!

"Dude!" he exclaimed to Kevin. "You cut that really close! Mickey almost ate us alive!"

But Kevin didn't react. Instead he approached me and put his arm around my shoulder.

"You okay?" he asked seriously.

I swallowed hard.

"Why? What do you mean? Of course I'm okay. I'm fine," I lied and cursed myself a moment later. Why didn't I just say something? My friends had just proved they trusted me and that I could trust them. They had risked their lives for me. Why didn't I return the favor? I didn't know. All I could think about was the note Mickey had secretly shoved in my hand just before he stormed off.

A Thief in the *Devil's Pit*

"No worries, we'll meet again, loser." I could still hear the ominous echo of Mickey the bulldozer in my head.

I had locked myself in the boys' bathroom at school and stared at the piece of paper in my hand. Barely legible, badly spelled handwriting threatened me:

"Totay at three at thee olld ruin in the forest. On we'll gett un little broten.

Fear crept down my spine. What should I do? There wouldn't always be a principal to show up at the right place at the right time to save us from the *Unbeatables*.

And I sure couldn't drag the *Wild Soccer Bunch* into this. This had nothing to do with soccer. They had their stadium, their *Devil's Pit,* their real life floodlights and they were proud of them all. And tomorrow they'd have their first game. I couldn't steal this from them.

But at the same time, I felt outside of it all, like I wasn't a part of the team anymore. I felt outside of everything. I was alone. And all I could think about was my brother. I had to protect him. I had to keep Josh out of this. This was all my fault. I'm the one who went to the Graffiti Towers. I'm the one who made a pact with Mickey the bulldozer. My mom always said I have to keep my promises. Besides, what I was thinking and what I was about to do – maybe this was where I belonged now; maybe I was not being good enough to hang with the *Wild Soccer Bunch* any more. I went to the Graffiti Towers looking for my father. If he really lived there, then maybe that was where I belonged too.

The first bell rang. Class would start soon. I threw the note into the toilet, flushed it, and then ran out into the hallway as if nothing had happened.

In class I played good old Julian Fort Knox. But in reality I was looking for the slightest chance to escape from this life forever. I was thinking crazy, I knew it, but I didn't see a way out.

Nothing was easy. When I was a little kid, everything was easy. So when did everything turn so hard? My friends took good care of me, especially Zoe, Tyler, and Fabio. I was never alone, not even for a second, and it was a miracle that I was able to hide my cleats under my desk without them noticing.

The final bell rang so loud in my head, I jumped a mile. Everyone grabbed their bags and ran into the playground. Practice time! This would be our last training at the *Devil's Pit* before the big game. The bike racks were crowded when I got there.

"Oh shoot!" I said. "I left my cleats at home!" I said, desperately putting on my best performance.

The others looked at me as if I had left my head at home.

"I know, what a pain," I said, pretending to be embarrassed. "I'll just go home and get them. Meet you at the *Devil's Pit* in 20 minutes. Promise!"

No one said a word.

"What?" I asked. "You know, I really should go."

Danny spoke first.

"What's your shoe size?"

"Who, me?"

"No, the other guy living in your clothes," said Danny. "Of *course* you!"

"I wear a 5," I confessed.

"Good. I have the same size," Fabio smiled. "And I brought two pairs."

"Wait, what?" I stammered. "I don't think I got all of that."

I stared into their faces, shocked. But they all smiled back at me.

"It's a no-brainer, Julian. You can wear Fabio's extra pair of shoes," Zoe explained, as if it was the most natural thing in the world. "So, can we go now? Julian, you lead."

I froze. On the one hand, this was an incredible honor; to lead, I mean! The front of the *Wild Soccer Bunch* bike caravan was always Zoe's spot. She was the best biker on the team, after all. She set the pace, and on top of the hill just before the stadium, she signaled the final sprint down the hill. We all knew she'd give up the top spot only if someone beat her... which would only happen if she rode with two broken legs. Even Kevin and Danny, who were our leads in different situations, had never been allowed to ride in the lead. They'd asked, but she had always turned them down, no ifs, ands, or buts.

They complained now, too, but nobody dared to criticize Zoe's suggestion. As far as bike riding goes, she was top dog.

Without further ado, she shoved me toward my bike. I

took the hint and a few seconds later, I raced out onto the street at the front of the *Wild Soccer Bunch* bike caravan. Honestly, I didn't feel honored at all. In fact, I felt like a frog under a microscope, with its beating heart on display. I felt X-rayed and gamma rayed. I felt my friends' eyes burn holes into the back of my head, and I feared they could see the dark secrets of my soul. In other words, I was a total mess. What else is new?

I tromped down on the pedals as if I was chased by wild killer bees. Why did they do this to me? I thought they were my friends, but it was clear that they didn't trust me any more. They wanted me to ride up front so they could keep an eye on me; they were afraid I was going to run away with the money. Was I being paranoid? No, more like my conscience wouldn't shut up. Money was the last thing on my mind. I was worried about my brother. How could I protect him? I heard my mom's voice in my head again, so I raced like crazy up that hill ahead of the *Wild Soccer Bunch,* because my secrets were making me sick!

I sped up even more. I just wanted to get away from everything. I was ashamed. I was angry with everyone and everything. Not for a second did I consider that my friends wanted to help me. Even the extra pair of cleats was proof of their distrust. They wanted to make sure

I didn't go home. And the way they came to the rescue this morning? Did they really save me from Mickey? No! Oh no! You don't believe that, do you? No, they just wanted to make sure he didn't get our money. I mean *their* money. My anger grew. I pedaled even faster, and when I reached the top of the hill overlooking the stadium, I yelled as loud as I could:

"Sprint!"

The wooden fence around our soccer field shot towards me. Zoe and Tyler were in hot pursuit on my right and on my left. But they couldn't pass me. I was too fast. I pulled both brakes so I wouldn't crash into the fence. Dust whirled around me and engulfed me, pebbles flew through the air, my bike reared, and I did a 180. Then I just stood there, waiting until a nanosecond later. Zoe's and Tyler's bikes reared like ponies and came to a halt right next to me.

They looked at me and didn't say a word until the rest of the *Wild Soccer Bunch* stopped their bikes next to us. Then Zoe whistled through her teeth and Tyler murmured: "Wow!"

"That was really wild!" Danny whispered and Tyler looked at me. "Nobody's ever done that before."

"Outstanding, dude, you beat Zoe!" Roger shouted. I couldn't believe it.

Zoe nodded respectfully at me. She was too exhausted to do anything else. Tyler was just as exhausted. "Julian, that was a monumental sprint! All the way from school to the *Devil's Pit*. Nobody has ever done that before."

I grinned. Maybe life wasn't so bad after all.

"Is that true?" I could barely believe it.

"Yeah, unfortunately," Zoe laughed at me. "But it's a loss I'm willing to take because I have never seen anybody ride that fast before."

I blushed. My face was like a lighthouse in the fog, but I didn't care. None of my friends seemed to care either, and together we pushed our bikes into the *Devil's Pit,* the one and only stadium the *Wild Soccer Bunch* ever wants to play in.

Larry was waiting for us, and our joyous mood was contagious. Usually cranky and with a face as withered as his jacket, he greeted us with a suggestion that never ever had crossed his mind before, let alone his lips: "Let's just scrimmage today!" he shouted and kicked the ball in the air.

"Defenders against forwards! Julian, Alexander, Tyler, Josh, Kyle, and Zoe play Joey, Kevin, Danny, Diego, Fabio, and Roger."

No one moved. They couldn't believe what they were hearing.

"What are you waiting for?"

What were we waiting for? Absolutely nothing!

We dropped our bikes to the ground, piled our pants, jackets, shoes, and sweaters into the mix and minutes later, we stood on the field in full uniform. Except me. I wore my street pants, obviously. The Larry birthday present money bank vault was staying with me.

Then we started the game.

Diego just tipped the ball and Kevin stopped it. I thought he'd play it back to Fabio who on his turn would send Danny, our fastest mid-fielder dangerously close to our goal. So I ran towards Danny to cover him, and Tyler ran past Kevin to stop Fabio's pass. But Tyler walked into nothing. The pass never happened. Kevin hadn't even stopped the ball. He just caressed the ball with the tip of his cleats, and then he accelerated.

Kevin was fast, and before Tyler realized what his brother was planning, Kevin had passed Zoe. Alex, too, slid into nothing as Kevin slalom-dribbled past him. I had no choice but to run back into the penalty area.

Fire on my heels, I raced over the field. Could I prevent the goal? Kyle the invincible came too far out of the goal and threw himself into Kevin. But Kevin just lifted the ball over Kyle's fists, jumped over him, and won it back. I knew we were doomed. Kevin could score easily, but for whatever reason, decided not to kick the ball into the empty goal where Josh was on guard like a furious watchdog, covering for our missing goalie. This gave me time to approach from the right. Kevin glared at me, but didn't hesitate a second, not even for one-hundredth of a heartbeat.

He prepared the very best lightning passes; everyone knew that. And that's why he heeled the ball back and to the left, because he knew where every one of his teammates were by pure instinct. Joey, who was always behind him and slightly to the left, intercepted the perfect pass, moved the ball to the left, and was about to shoot off toward the goal.

But not so fast! I, Julian Fort Knox, the all-in-one defender, made a clean and perfect slide towards Joey's legs and made it impossible for him to shoot. But he was quick enough to release the ball to Fabio, who was trying to steal it. Fabio didn't like things easy, and a direct shot to the goal was too easy. He stopped the ball first with his chest and lifted it above his head with his knee. He was about to bid the ball farewell and send it into the net, when I crashed his party. The all-in-one defender stole the ball from his shoe, played around Danny, forced the ball forward a few more feet, and then passed a deadly shot to Tyler. He was lurking at the halfway line, took off with the ball, and no matter how much Kevin, Fabio, Joey, and Danny yelled, they couldn't catch him. All our hopes rested on Diego and Roger. They were in Tyler's way. But Zoe came from the left. Since her birthday tournament, she and Tyler were a team as if they were born to play together.

Without any trouble, Tyler passed the ball to her. She passed back to him and they continued passing to each other four times while Diego and Roger practiced zigzagging after the two of them. Finally, Zoe, who got the last pass from Tyler, just hit the ball hard from close range and the ball slammed into the far corner of the net!

Oh, I will tell you, life was beautiful! The Graffiti Towers and Mickey the bulldozer had ceased to exist. All that mattered was the *Devil's Pit*, my friends, the *Wild Soccer Bunch*, and tomorrow's game.

After practice, we gathered at the kiosk for our ritual lemonade. Danny whispered into my ear: "Tonight, midnight, surprise birthday party for Larry."

For a split second I had no idea what he was talking about.

"Pass it on!" he whispered again.

That's when I woke up and reality hit me like a sledgehammer: Larry's birthday present; the second-hand shop we'd go to in a few minutes; the money in my pants that would be gone forever. There were no easy-popping balloons after all; no, the *Unbeatables* were real. Mickey's bullying words burned into me and I could see his note even though I had flushed it down the toilet back at school. Who would protect Josh? Only the money could save him and I was his big brother and I couldn't let anything happen to him. I couldn't let them spend the money. I had to prevent the trip to the store at any cost.

"Come on, pass it on!" Danny hissed again, but instead of passing it on, I jumped up, ran to my bike, and raced off.

Danny looked at Tyler and Tyler looked at Zoe. She looked at Kevin and he nodded.

"Yes, but don't go too fast!" he said. "If he sees you, it's all over."

Larry raised an eyebrow. He had no clue what they were talking about. After all, he knew nothing about Mickey the bulldozer or the birthday money in my pocket. But Larry never treated us like children. He understood that we had to solve some of our problems ourselves, and this seemed to be one of them. He respected that. And so he just watched as Zoe took off, following me. Even if Larry had known what lay ahead, he would never stop us.

The Worst Day of My Life

Nice chapter title, right? Well, it's true.

Larry wouldn't have stopped us, but I wanted him to.
I wanted Larry to step in and stop what was about to
happen. And I'm asking each and every one of you for
your forgiveness. Those of you who followed my request
and swore the oath. Those of you who bookmarked the
page with the oath. I'm sorry to each and every one of
you who trusted me. You trusted me even though you
didn't even know me and even though you didn't know
my father. You trusted me because you know that I am
one of the *Wild Soccer Bunch*.

There you have it, in writing. Honestly, I don't
deserve to be one of the *Wild Soccer Bunch*. Go on! Close
the book, flatten the bookmark, and give this book away
as a present to your worst enemy. A book that teaches
you how to let down your friends is only good for one
thing. Enemies.

Not only had I stolen my friends' money; not only
had I messed up Larry's birthday surprise; now I had

deserted my team just before the first game in the *Devil's Pit,* the stadium of the *Wild Soccer Bunch a.u.,* which, in case you forgot, means "Always United." I had been proud of this once, too; so proud, in fact, that I went to the Graffiti Towers to tell my father. And look what it got me. I had to straighten this out. Just me.

My bad conscience pushed me forward. I rode even faster than I did on the way to practice. I raced along streets, jumped up and down curbs and sidewalks, and like a Native American horseman, I hung to the side so I could fit under the gate to the Grim Woods.

I steered my bike into the brush and disappeared from the eyes of the world. I jumped over roots and stones, cowered under twigs, and finally reached the old house ruins. I stepped on the brakes, reared my bike like a horse, did a wheelie, and looked at the ruins. The broken archway looked like a devil's claw. The view sent shivers down my spine.

I may have been a traitor to my team, but I was still a human being, with pride, heart, and determination.

"Hey, Mickey!" I shouted. "I know you're out there! I can smell you, you hear? In fact, I can smell all of you!"

It was eerily quiet for a moment, but then they came out. One by one, they crawled out of the shadows around me: Mow-down, Humungous, Juggernaut, Grim Reaper, Octopus, and Kong. They wore twigs and tall weeds on their backs as camouflage. And finally their leader appeared as well. A shower of stones dropped from the archway, which moaned underneath his weight. Mickey the bulldozer showed himself, dark and black against the sky. With that ominous view, my front wheel hit the dust in front of him.

"Where's the money?" he asked and the question was like a slap in my face.

Zoe could feel it too. What I didn't know then was that she was hiding in the bushes, watching; I found that out later. She watched me pull out my cap with the money inside. She watched the whole thing.

"Here!" I held it out to him, hatred in my voice. "Here is your money. But I'm warning you, Fatso. If Josh has even a scratch on him, I will turn you into fertilizer!"

Mickey the bulldozer just stared at me. His beady eyes burned and almost forced me to my knees. But I fought the impulse. He laughed; he doubled over he laughed so hard. And that's when his gang jumped me, pinned me to the ground, and took the money from me.

All I could think was, "Thank God, it's finally over."

But I was as wrong as showing up in the wrong town for a soccer game.

Octopus and Kong pulled me to my feet and held me tight.

"Let go of me!" I shouted, as brave as a sardine staring down a whale.

"You're coming with us," Mickey decided as he heaved his body off the archway. "You didn't want to go home anyway, did you?"

He slid down the archway, loosening so many stones that I was sure it would come crashing down. It didn't.

"You really think anyone is going to miss you after what you've done today?"

Mickey the bulldozer leaned in on me and grinned. His beady eyes hit my heart and stopped it for at least ten seconds.

"This is it," I thought. The coin had hit the ground and the side up was the side of the *Unbeatables*.

I couldn't and didn't want to believe it. The all-in-one defender was defenseless. And when Mickey gave the order to move on, I marched along with them like a good little soldier. I marched with him into their world, which from now on would be my world: the other side of the Grim Woods. My old world, the world of the *Wild Soccer Bunch,* had ceased to exist.

As they took me away, I looked back and caught a glimpse of Zoe, standing there among the tall weeds. She looked helpless and bit her lips in anger; her dark eyes glowed like fire. But then she saw the coin at her feet. It was my lucky coin, and she recognized it immediately. We tossed it in the air before every game to decide who got first kick and who played which side. Matching Mickey's contempt when tossing it away, Zoe picked it up gingerly and gently brushed it off with her shirt. That was the last I saw of her.

At the End of the World

Mickey the bulldozer, his *Unbeatables,* and I left the Grim Woods. We marched through the tall weeds across the Prairie and reached a point I didn't even know existed. Although the Graffiti Towers were to our far left already, we still moved further and further away. We walked across a different section of the desolate Prairie like a horde of nomads until we were all alone. Even the Grim Woods, the last familiar reference point connecting me to my old life, disappeared behind the horizon. The sun would soon follow.

Night was about to fall and I was walking into no man's land. I felt as if I was swimming in 10,000 feet of water, surrounded by sharks. I couldn't think of a worse place to be on Earth. Then we marched up a hill, and I soon learned that I was wrong.

Mickey and his gang seemed to be quite happy. They were obviously proud of whatever they were going to show me. Excuse me, but I couldn't share their excitement. I was totally appalled.

I looked down the hill at a rundown trailer park made up of old RVs and corrugated huts and rickety wooden shacks. Neon lights swung in the wind, illuminating stolen cars that were being dismantled with hissing welding torches and power tools. Dark and sinister men and women scurried about, whispering and snickering. I had heard about this place before but I never really believed it existed until that very moment that I looked down on it. It was called "Outlaw's Nest." Make no mistake about it: this was not a place for the likes of you – or me.

Then I saw him. He was sitting in one of the huts, counting money, in the light of a bare bulb. He was as big as Jabba the Hut. In an instant I knew who he was: the boss. Mickey's cousin. He was so large and blubbery, he made Mickey look like a young Abe Lincoln.

The *Unbeatables* smiled at each other as if what lay below us was the realization of all their dreams. One day they all wanted to be just like that disgusting criminal down there, sitting under a bare bulb, drooling over a pile of cash. They took a deep breath, spit on the ground, and tried to summon up their courage before descending the hill.

Mickey grabbed my arm. "Now that you've seen it," he announced pompously, "you're gonna keep your mouth shut. There's no turning back now. Guard this secret with your life – and I *do* mean *life*. Got that?"

Then he squeezed me so hard I thought I was going to die.

"Got it?" he hissed again. I nodded, and he let go immediately.

"See? What did I tell you? I've always liked this dwarf. He's one of us now! Go on, give him a nice welcome!" he laughed and put his hubcap hands on my shoulder.

The other *Unbeatables* followed his signal. One after the other passed by me and smiled before they went down the hill.

I stayed back. Just me and the Grim Reaper. He suspiciously circled around me, looking at his prize like he'd just turned me over to the Dark Side.

"Mickey might trust you, but I don't. This is the only warning you're gonna get," he murmured. "I got my eye on you."

"Oh really?" There I went again. I never knew when to keep my mouth shut. My mom always said it and there I was, about to pop off again. "Which eye would that be?"

The Grim Reaper didn't expect that. They never do. I could see in his eyes that some brain cells were firing off, trying to make heads or tails of what I was saying, but they just didn't connect. They couldn't connect. There just weren't enough of them. "You heard me, *Defenderless*," he hissed. This guy really had no sense of humor. "I will hurt and torture you if you double-cross us. Is that clear?"

I nodded like a good little soldier. Then I ran down the hill. Compared to the Grim Reaper's company even the *Outlaw's Nest* seemed like a monastery. The morons who were already there were greeted as if they were a bunch of cuddly toy animals. Kiss here and hug there. Even I was greeted that way. Yuck! But for the first time I felt absolutely safe, too. I was definitely at the end of the world. I was in hell and the devil himself had just kissed and hugged me. I couldn't think of anything worse that could happen to me. Right?

"Hey, big guy!" Mickey greeted his cousin. "I have

money for you. Here you go!"

He poured the money on the table.

"It's $221. And for that I want the best; the best of the best. It's party time!"

Mickey the bulldozer and his cousin grinned at each other.

"That's a big ten-four deal, bro," the fat king of thieves said. "Let's use $71 for the party. I'll keep the rest. Like I'm your bank. You have to start thinking about the future, bro. The wind is getting colder, and winter is just around the corner."

"Okay by me. If you think that's the way to go." Mickey shrugged.

Then he turned around. Behind us the gate of one of the corrugated iron huts opened and revealed a truckload of the finest candy. But more amazing than any candy was the person standing in the gate. It was one of Mickey's girl cousins. Wow! I had never seen anyone like her. Of course, I didn't know too many girls, but I knew Zoe – and this girl was nothing like her.

The *Wild Bunch*

The way they told it, Zoe was even wilder than usual
when she arrived at Camelot. In fact, she was downright
agitated. The *Wild Soccer Bunch* had gathered in the tree
house just before nine o'clock. Even Larry was there,
although it would be his birthday in just a few hours.
He was turning the big 4-0. But he wasn't thinking
about celebrating. Just like the others, he was listening
to Zoe's report. Standing tall in the center of Camelot,
she was trying to contain her fury.

"Danny, you were right!" she stated bitterly. "Julian is
being blackmailed by Mickey the bulldozer."

Murmurs and hisses filled the hall on the ground floor
of the tree house. Josh didn't know what blackmail
meant, so Kevin explained it to him.

"If Julian had not given him the money for Larry's
birthday present, Mickey would have grabbed Josh."

More murmurs and hisses. The *Wild Soccer Bunch*
balled their fists. Josh looked up at Zoe.

"But where is Julian now?" He sounded desperate.

Zoe didn't answer. She bit her lip. Then she spoke so softly as if she didn't want to hear her words herself.

"They took him. Beyond the Grim Woods, even beyond the Prairie!"

They all sucked in a breath, shocked.

Nobody had expected that. The Prairie was not part of the world of the *Wild Soccer Bunch*. It was the world of their sworn enemies, the *Unbeatables*. The *Wild Soccer Bunch* had no power there, and none of them had ever dared to even go there. But as the church bell rang midnight, their fate was sealed.

Josh wiped the tears off his face and looked at Kevin and Danny. But even the wildest of the *Wild Soccer Bunch* were paralyzed. This had nothing to do with soccer. This wasn't a game any more. This was serious. It was beyond serious. It was terrifying. It was beyond anything any of them had ever experienced.

Kevin the star striker, a guy who wasn't afraid of anything, pushed his fingernails into his palms until the pain was too much to bear; he hit the wall with his fist.

Danny, the world's fastest midfielder, bit his fingernails.

Zoe the fearless looked at Tyler, our number 10, the heart and soul and inspiration of the *Wild Soccer Bunch*.

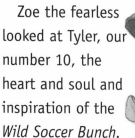

Not even Tyler had an answer. He looked to Fabio the wizard.

But Fabio, son of soccer God, Ribaldo of the *Furies*, couldn't think of anything either and started to pray.

Kyle the invincible was no longer invincible and Joey the magician was so consumed by fear that you could almost see his magic float away.

Diego the tornado fought his asthma, a sure sign he was scared, while Roger the hero paced anxiously, tearing at his hair, speechless. It was as if he had lost his voice, just like Alex.

But Alex the cannon  Alexander was the only one of the *Wild Soccer Bunch* who wasn't about to be scared off. He looked to Larry, the best coach in the world, struggled and struggled and then said more than he had in two years. "Forget the *Devil's Pit* and the league. Julian is our friend and I won't play without him."

Larry met Alex's glance. Slowly a smile began playing around Larry's mouth and his eyes beamed with joy.

"Thanks, Alex," he said. "This is the nicest birthday present anyone's ever given me."

Alex smiled, too, but the rest of the *Wild Soccer Bunch* didn't get it. What did Larry mean? They had already lost me, now they were supposed to give up on everything else, too? Everything they cared so much about? Their team, the *Devil's Pit,* and the league? Larry couldn't seriously expect this. But Larry silenced their protests. He pushed back his baseball cap and scratched his forehead. He always did that when he was serious.

"Well," he began, "I'd like to help you. I mean if you let me. I am your coach, and this has to do with soccer, too. Unless you are ready to skip tomorrow's game."

He looked at the *Wild Soccer Bunch* and waited until the spark of understanding and relief filled the room.

"Okay," he nodded. "Glad you're ready to fight. I knew you would be, and so I came prepared. Let me show you."

Larry got up and the *Wild Soccer Bunch* followed. He asked them to wait in front of the tree house as he left the yard. Ten minutes later he came back on his moped. It moaned and groaned as it pulled a trailer behind it with a sky-high load.

Larry stopped in front of the tree house, turned off the moped, and looked at his team.

"This should work. Kevin, Danny, Zoe, and Tyler! You ride to the Grim Woods and get Julian's bike. Then you find Mickey and challenge him. But *really* challenge him, you know what I mean? Tease him. Get him angry. Get him all dazed and confused. Then grab Julian and come back here. Mickey will follow you. Make sure of that. Got it?"

Kevin, Danny, Zoe, and Tyler did their best to swallow their fear.

They nodded at first but then someone said "No, we didn't get it. Can you repeat that?"

"No, I can't," Larry said. "We don't have enough time. We have to make Camelot a fortress. Fabio, Diego, Alex, Josh, Roger, Kyle, and Joey! Come on, help me."

He pulled the tarp off his trailer and revealed a collection of trash cans, water guns, nets, rope, soap, a steamer, an electric pump, a bag of feathers and a huge pot of honey.

The *Wild Soccer Bunch* stared at him. Kevin did this funny thing with his eyebrows whenever he was deep in thought.

"What kind of fortress do you have in mind?" he asked skeptically.

"The best fortress in the world. Mickey won't show up alone and he won't show up unarmed. We have to be prepared for anything."

The *Wild Soccer Bunch* froze. Honey, soap, and feathers against the *Unbeatables,* who'd show up with bats and chains? They might as well turn the *Devil's Pit* into a miniature golf course.

But Larry was serious. He was already unloading his trailer.

"What's up? What are you waiting for? Let's be prepared or Mickey will come and kidnap you just like he did Julian and take you to the Prairie!"

"Excuse me? Did I just hear you correctly?" asked a voice that seemed a bit out of place among the *Wild Soccer Bunch.* Larry turned around and there was my mom, coming out of the kitchen.

"Where did you say my son was? Who took whom to the Prairie?"

Larry paced, pushed his baseball cap into his neck three times, and finally scratched his forehead.

"Well, I don't know if you should get involved. You might get upset. Then again you might want to help us."

My mother crinkled her nose. Her expression grew dark. The volcano was about to erupt. Josh knew instantly what was coming. But he also knew that you cannot stop a volcano from erupting. Unless you are Larry, the best coach in the world.

"So what do you say?" Larry asked. "Will you help us?"

When Larry told me what my mom did next, it blew my mind. She nodded. She agreed to help! But she looked worried. Larry reassured her, rummaged in his toolbox, and slapped an electric screwdriver in her open hand. "I'll explain on the way. Let's go boys and girls."

Someone asked, "But what about the game?" and Larry said, "I postponed it." Then he turned to the rest of the *Wild Soccer Bunch* and grinned: "That's what floodlights are for!"

On a Tightrope

The howling wind carried the ten chimes of the church bell all the way to the Prairie. Clouds raced along the sky and the smell of fall hung in the air. But the *Unbeatables* didn't seem to notice or care. They bounced and tossed and waved the bags they got at the Outlaw's Nest, roaring and hollering. The three girl cousins giggled. Or rather, the two who looked like Mickey, giggled.

The third girl was different. She walked quietly along with us, stealing an occasional glance at me. Yech. Why did she do that? And why did I get that weird feeling in my stomach when she did?

I tried to ignore her. But I didn't have to look at her to see her eyes, her long brown hair, and her face. As we walked along, she came closer and closer to me and when she accidentally bumped into me, I shivered.

It scared me, but it also made me feel better. The red eyes of the rats scurrying around us now looked like harmless glowworms. The fall wind felt refreshing and I was almost glad to be here on the Prairie and not in the

Devil's Pit or at Camelot.

I realized that this must have been what my mom and dad felt before the Grim Woods separated them.

I felt light. The Graffiti Towers appeared on the horizon and they no longer looked scary or foreboding.

At the same time, I was told later that Danny, Zoe, and Kevin stood near the ruins in the Grim Woods and tied my bike to Tyler's back. Then they all jumped on their mountain bikes and rode through the high weeds onto the Prairie. The clouds raced above them and with serious expressions on their faces, they fought the wind as they took the usual route to the Graffiti Towers.

Suddenly Zoe pointed at the right tower.

"There! Do you see it? What is that?"

One shooting star after another crossed the sky. I saw them too.

At another part of the Prairie, Mickey the Bulldozer saw the same thing.

"Woweee!" howled Mickey the bulldozer and "Woweee-ee-ee!" came the echo of the *Unbeatables*.

We stood in front of an old out of service power pole and looked up at Octopus. The guy with the Mohawk, Grim Reaper, was swinging on the pole 20 feet above the ground, pulling up a rope with one of the candy bags tied to the end. He took it off and fastened it on a hook. When he let go, the bag started to slide along a steel cable, accelerating, going faster and faster, all the way to the next power pole about 100 feet away where an old warehouse was squatting in the dark like a giant tombstone. The sparks in its wake lit the night sky like shooting stars.

"Woweee!" Mickey howled again and "Woweee-ee-ee!" came the echo of the *Unbeatables*.

The girl next to me laughed and I joined in. Every time a bag raced along the cable we closed our eyes and made a wish. My wish was always the same: that my father would come to the *Devil's Pit* and see me play. Fat chance of *that* happening. It seemed like good things didn't happen to me anymore, so there was no way my wish would come true. Even if I did find my father here, I'd never be one of the *Wild Soccer Bunch* again.

Mickey's voice cut through my thoughts.

"Hey, *Defenderless!*" he yelled. "Your turn!"

I stared at him. He couldn't be serious. The power pole was twice as high as the old bridge we jumped off before the game against the *Furies*. And there was no water under the pole; nothing to soften a fall. Give me a break! This was no dare. This was crazy!

"What's the matter, loser?" Mickey yelled. "I thought you were one of us now. That's what you wanted, right?"

I just glared at him. This guy was totally nuts.

"Thought so," Mickey rambled on. "Well, prove it. Consider this your test. Like trying out for a new team. Make sense?"

No, it didn't make any sense at all, but neither did anything else in my life right now, so I swallowed hard. I was scared like never before but there was no turning back. With a last glance at the girl, I climbed up the power pole.

Octopus was already up there, waiting for me. He had a sadistic grin on his face when he handed me the wire with the two wooden handles.

"Let her rip!" he said. "Slide down the steel cable all the way to the warehouse! See the bags? Just like them!"

I nodded.

"That's where the cable goes back up," he went on. "Wait until you slow down, right after you pass the warehouse."

"Then what?" I asked, already knowing the answer.

He grinned. "Then you let go!" Then after an ominous pause he added, "But don't wait too long."

"W-why not?" I asked. "If I go too far I'll just come back, right?"

"Not a chance," Octopus grinned. "Any idea what happens to the plastic bags over there?"

I didn't, of course, and I had no clue what he was getting at. Octopus grabbed the last bag with candy, hung it on the cable and let it go, and like a shooting star, it raced down to the warehouse and beyond.

"Keep your eyes on the bag!" Octopus reminded me.

I squinted and then I saw it. Just before the next power pole, a three-foot metal beam attached to the steel cable, automatically disconnected the hook from the cable. The bag twirled off the cable and crashed straight into a concrete wall.

"BAM!" Octopus explained, "Timing is everything. If I were you, I'd let go."

I swallowed hard and looked down at Mickey standing below me. Doing this was my only chance, so I threw the handles over the steel cable and jumped.

"I am Julian Fort Knox the all-in-one defenderrrrr!" I yelled as loud as I could, and with a trail of sparks behind me like the tail of a comet, high above the ground, I raced across the Prairie. The warehouse and the wall of doom flew at me incredibly fast.

"Oh boy, oh boy, oh boy, oh boy," I repeated over and over to myself as the wind rushed over my face and the warehouse loomed large.

The metal beam that would disconnect my handles from the cable raced toward me. There was no stopping

this. I would have to jump or I'd be thrown straight at the wall. One-Two-Three-WILD! And I let go!

I saw the large pile of cardboard boxes right underneath me and when I let go, there was a long, weightless drop, then WHAM! I crashed into them.

Lying on my back, for a moment I thought I was dead. But then somebody called my name and at first I thought it was an angel. No, the voice was familiar. It was one of the *Wild Soccer Bunch!* Then there were more voices shouting at me. I shook the cobwebs out of my head. It was four of the wildest guys in the whole wide world!

"Julian! Julian, where are you? Dude! We have to get out of here!" they yelled as they dug through the cardboard boxes, looking for me.

I was paralyzed. Where did they come from? And what did they want? Did they just want their money? Or did they want me? After all, I was a thief. Wasn't I?

Four faces appeared right above me: Kevin, Tyler, Danny, and Zoe.

"Why didn't you say anything?! Julian, thank God you're alive. We need you. We can't play in the *Devil's Pit* without our all-in-one defender! We wouldn't play without you. Ever."

Wait a minute. Did I just hear what I thought I heard? I was totally confused. "Do you really mean that?" I said, crawling out. I was overwhelmed.

That's when the Grim Reaper appeared above us. He jumped straight into the cardboard boxes, got up quickly, and began pummeling me: "I knew it! You're nothing but a stinking little traitor!"

Kevin, Danny, and Tyler jumped on him and tied his hands behind his back with his own bicycle chain and shoved a paper bag over his head. "What's this weirdo talking about?" Kevin asked.

"He's out there where the buses don't run," I answered. "They all are. They thought I joined their team."

We all laughed uproariously at how dumb the whole thing was and how utterly ridiculous Grim Reaper looked, all tied up with a bag over his head.

"Let's get out of here!" Kevin said, grabbing me. "This place gives me the creeps!" And together we ran to our bikes. They were loaded with the plastic bags from the Outlaw's Nest.

A hiss announced the next *Unbeatable* on the steel cable. Judging by the huge shadow, it had to be Mickey himself.

"Hurry!" Kevin rushed us along, but the *Unbeatables* had beat us to it and blocked our retreat, standing guard right behind our bikes, holding them hostage.

Then Mickey the bulldozer crashed into the pile of boxes.

This was it. The end of the line for *Wild Soccer Bunch* defense.

Suddenly the headlights of a familiar pick-up truck lit up the night. It screeched to a stop right in front of us.

"Come on!" I said. "They won't hurt us any more!" And as if in response to what I said, the driver got out of the truck.

He just stood there, tall and imposing, and watched

us run to our bikes. The *Unbeatables* didn't move a muscle and silently watched us disappear across the Prairie. When we reached the other side, we stopped and looked back at Mickey and the *Unbeatables*.

Mickey exploded. He noticed Grim Reaper on the ground, desperately trying to pull the paper bag off his head. On the bag, Tyler had drawn a perfect rendition of the *Wild Soccer Bunch* logo and the words, "Don't mess with the *Wild Soccer Bunch!*"

Mickey screamed louder than I'd ever heard him, loud enough to be heard in Peoria. "This isn't over, you twerps! We're coming for you tonight! We know where you hang out, *Defenderless*. We'll show you what we do to traitors!"

"That guy is delusional," Kevin laughed.

I didn't think it was so funny. I knew he meant it. I guess we all did. We knew they would come to Camelot, and we raced off to prepare for battle.

The Battle for Camelot

With Mickey's threat at our backs, we flew over the Prairie and through the Grim Woods and we didn't hit the brakes until we got to Dearborn Street. "Larry!" we yelled up at the tree house. "It worked. They're on their way!"

Everything got real quiet and everyone who was working at Camelot stopped their tools, except for my mother's electric drill. She accidentally pressed the button on the handle and didn't let go and it whined and whined. She didn't even notice it when she demanded an explanation. I could see she had been terribly worried and I went to her and hugged her. Neither of us said a word for a moment or two. All I heard was the whining of the electric drill in my ear.

Larry gently took the drill from my mother's hand. "I think it's best if we go inside."

My mother looked at him, kind of wild. She wanted to say something else, but Larry stopped her.

"It's okay, Mrs. Phillips. You helped a lot. But now it's time to let the *Wild Soccer Bunch* do what they have to do."

My mother hesitated. She looked long and hard at me, and finally managed a smile. I could see that she was fighting with herself, just like I had been fighting with myself. I think we both won that night. She did something only the world's best mother can do. She nodded and without another word she followed Larry inside.

We waited until they were gone. Then we took our positions. Mickey the Bulldozer and his *Unbeatables* were really bad characters and we had to make a stand against their bullying, once and for all.

It was quiet after 10 o'clock. Even the wind had died down. Zoe, who sat next to me on the second floor of Camelot, looked at me, biting her lip.

"I'm scared."

"I know," I nodded. "Everyone is, including me." I paused. "Especially me."

I tried to smile, and so did she.

"No worries. I won't tell anyone," she whispered. "And I'm super glad you are back with us, Julian Fort Knox, our very own all-in-one defender. That's really a mouthful. We should work on that name. Fine tune it."

Suddenly a blood curdling howl filled the air. "Arroooo!"

Then the fence moaned and the garden door fell closed. Three racing heartbeats later, the shadows of the

Unbeatables peeled out of the dark night, armed to the teeth with crowbars, bicycle chains, and baseball bats that glistened in the moonlight.

"Arroooo!" Mickey the bulldozer lifted his arm and stopped his gang.

He looked around suspiciously, barely 30 feet away from us. After all, this wouldn't have been the first time he'd lose out against us. But this time everything was in his favor. And we all knew it.

"Hello! Anyone home?" he yelled and took three steps forward. He seemed more amused than anything else. He was not even armed.

"I'm looking for the wild soccer dweebs. Are they here? Or are they hiding behind their mommy?"

He laughed. We steamed.

"Just you wait," Fabio hissed. Then he said something in Portuguese. We had no idea what it was, but when he was done, he seemed satisfied with himself. We were pretty sure whatever it was, it was about Mickey and it wasn't nice.

Roger lifted his water pistol ready to shoot, but Kevin held him back.

"No, not yet!" he murmured firmly.

"Well, when?" Fabio hissed. "It'll be too late when they attack."

"No, it won't be," Kevin said. "Trust the plan. I promise, none of these jerks will get to Camelot."

"Okay," Fabio said, unsure. "I hope you're right."

Mickey took another step closer.

"This is your last chance, boys and girls!" he announced as if he was some mafia boss. "Hand over the candy! It belongs to me! And give us Julian Fort Knox, the all-in-one defenseless, and nobody gets hurt."

That was the magic word. Josh got ready. It was his turn to protect me and he was ready for anything.

But wait! Before I continue telling the story, I have to ask a small favor of you. I know; I've been a disappointment so far. Twice I asked you to swear an oath and then I couldn't deliver. But this is not about me any more. It's about my friends. So please, do me the favor. Close the book, put your hand on the *Wild Soccer Bunch* logo, and observe a moment of silence. I want you to think about whether you want us to still be around tomorrow. And if you do, send all your good thoughts to the *Wild Soccer Bunch* now. They deserve it. I don't know anyone else who has done so much for me; anyone who has risked as much and forgiven so much. So please, do me the favor. We can use all the help we can get; because in all honesty, Kevin was the only one who thought that the *Unbeatables* would not reach the tree house. OMG!

"Hey, up there? Are you deaf?!" Mickey threatened again. "I'm not kidding, this is your very last chance. Hand over the candy and tell Julian to get down here! And we'll leave quietly. Otherwise–." I peered down at him through a knothole just as he ran a finger under his throat.

That's when Josh jumped up, angry as a crazed chipmunk. He was high up in Camelot's tower, the third

floor of our tree house, and yelled down to Mickey. "Hey moron, we won't let you go until you give us back our money! Fork it over now and we'll let you live!"

If I could have reached all the way up and high-fived my little brother, I would have done it, trust me on that.

Meanwhile, Mickey the bulldozer looked up at Josh, incredulous. Actually, he looked like a hungry alligator. He lifted his claw to signal attack, but at that exact same moment, Joey and Kyle pulled two switches on the lowest floor. Floodlights turned on everywhere and blinded the attackers.

"Help! I can't see! Turn off those lights!" The *Unbeatables* sounded really scared. Then Kevin opened fire.

Zoe, Fabio, Diego, and I appeared in the windows and hatches of Camelot and shot our super blasters at the staggering, blinded, *Unbeatables* and they ran around in circles like one foot was nailed to the floor, slamming into each other, everyone wailing like they were at nursery school during recess.

Mickey the bulldozer was blasted twice before he knew what hit him.

"*Unbeatables!* It's just squirt guns, you idiots! Re-group! Re-group! Let's go! Attack! Attack! We're not going to let a few puny squirt guns stop us!"

Mow-down, Juggernaut, and Humungous didn't need a reminder. With a horrifying battle cry, they lifted their crowbars and axes and stormed the doors of Camelot.

Tyler and Alex sat above them on the second floor veranda and like two puppeteers, they pulled a bunch of strings leading down to the ground underneath the tree house. Big blocks of wood suddenly appeared out of the grass, tripping Mow-down, Juggernaut, and Humungous and they fell flat on their faces. The earth shook as they hit the ground and their monstrous battle cries became squeaky screams of fear as they slid across the soap-covered tarp and twirled out of control right

at some tipped-over open trash cans! First Humungous slammed into the first one and got stuck headfirst, then Mow-Down, then Juggernaut. They didn't know what hit them and all three of them were hopelessly stuck inside. The last thing I heard was a chorus of terrified squeaky echoes coming from inside the trash cans, their feet sticking out and flapping like seals. I wanted to throw them a fish, but I had to get back to the battle.

Tyler and Alex high-fived each other and Danny bent over laughing. They almost didn't hear the warning from the tower.

"Grim Reaper and Octopus approaching at two o'clock! Danny! You're up!"

"Copy that!" Danny shouted. Josh was angry as a hornet, but Danny remained cool. Sitting in a fork in the tree, he waited for the jerks to attack. They swung their bats and crowbars. "Hey, dipstick!" Danny welcomed them. "Please make sure your tray tables are in an upright position and your seat belts are securely fastened!"

Octopus and Grim Reaper froze and stared up at Danny, who whipped out a pocket knife and cut the nylon cord in front of him.

"Enjoy your flight!" he said, as a sandbag dropped from the tree pulling a rope connected to a net that engulfed Octopus and Grim Reaper and pulled them up as fast as the sandbag fell down, trapping them in the net and suspending them 8 feet off the ground.

"Outstanding!" Danny was impressed. "That leaves only Kong, the giant prairie dog!"

He stared straight at Kong's butt. The jerk had crept up to the terrace without being seen. Now he was right in the middle of us. Tyler and Alex had no idea they were in imminent danger. Danny had to do something. But if he warned them, they might panic. Danny jumped out of his spot, leaped from the third to the second floor, and waved at Kong like he was sending him off to reform school.

"Hey, King Kong!" he yelled. "Didn't anyone teach you how to knock?"

Kong forgot about Tyler and Alex. He turned and furiously went for Danny, who ducked him like a bar of slippery soap, and led Kong to the hall, where a Kong-sized trap door was waiting for him. He fell right through it and slid down Josh's water slide and careened into the doghouse. Danny raced down and locked him in. "Nice doggy! If you're good, I'll get you fixed!" Kong, from inside the dog house, for the first time in his life, squealed like a frightened puppy.

The only one left was Mickey. He wasn't armed and

looked like easy pickings. But looks can be deceiving.

"Oh Mr. Bulldozer!" Roger called from somewhere in the tree house. "I can see you shaking from here! Are you cold? Or just scared? Do you want me to call your mommy? What do you want me to tell her?"

Mickey's beady little eyes twitched as his internal power supply glitched and looked like static on a TV screen. But then he turned on the brute force and his eyes turned into pinwheels, twirling in the night. At that moment, he looked like 200 pounds of unbridled, blubbering meanness!

Danny, still standing next to the doghouse, jumped up and climbed back up the tree.

"Stand by!" he yelled. "Mad dog in the house!"

Mickey spun around and heaved something heavy off his back and swung it onto his chest. Then he stood perfectly still. It looked like a Samsonite suitcase full of his dirty clothes and underwear. But I was wrong. He reached inside and slowly pulled out an electric drill with one hand, and a razor-sharp power saw blade with the other, and like he was jacking a clip into an automatic weapon, he snapped the saw blade into the drill with a terrifying CLANG. Then Mickey swung the case back over his shoulders and pulled the trigger on the saw-bladed drill. The razor-sharp blade whined to life and spun like a buzz-saw, glinting in the moonlight. Mickey stood his ground, looking like he just stepped out of a slasher movie.

"Kevin!" Danny whispered. "Kevin!"

No response. It was absolutely quiet except the roaring of Mickey's saw-bladed drill.

My mother tried to peer out the kitchen window, but Larry got in front of her and distracted her.

Mickey marched towards the wooden poles that held up Camelot. His saw-bladed drill would cut them in half like a knife going through butter.

We brought out the big guns and fired. Streams of water hit Mickey from every angle, but they didn't stop him. He didn't care and he laughed maniacally.

"Bring it on, punks!" He shouted. "I needed a bath anyway!"

"That's true," I said, reloading.

Mickey lifted the saw-bladed drill and prepared to make his first cut.

I knew that razor-sharp blade would turn Camelot to firewood. We had to stop him!

That's when Roger chimed in. The spinning buzz-saw of death was just a fraction of an inch away from the wood.

"Hey, Mickey!" he yelled from the scaffolding on the

second floor. "We have a surprise for you!" Next to him, a steamer hissed and a compressor rattled to life.

Mickey dumbly looked up and immediately recognized the danger. He was just about to say something that our parents would never let us say, when Roger fired, but instead of aiming straight at Mickey, he fired off a burst of ice water a good five feet above his head.

"Roger! What are you aiming at?" Zoe shouted to him.

"I was about to say the same thing!" Mickey laughed and readied his razor-sharp blade to cut our poles in half.

But Roger knew what he was doing. "Hey Mickwad! How about some dessert?"

Mickey looked up at Roger, puzzled. The he saw where Roger was looking and slowly raised his eyes up to what was happening directly over his head. There, about five feet above him was a wooden plank. Mickey still didn't get it and stayed where he was.

Suddenly Roger turned up the steam on the steamer and its jets of hot air pushed the wooden plank around, releasing a bucket, which tipped over and poured a gallon of thick honey all over Mickey's head and shoulders and dripped all the way down to his chubby little toes.

"Do you like honey on your filth?" Roger laughed and we all laughed uproariously.

Drenched in honey, Mickey let the drill with the razor-sharp saw blade drop to the ground, sawing off the ends of his shoes. He stuck his toes out to make sure they were still there and made a whimpering sound similar to the noise Kong made earlier. Assured that his toes were intact, he twirled and choked, but he couldn't make another sound. Finally he wiped the honey from his eyes and balled his fists at Roger. "I'll get you for this!" he sputtered through the thick honey.

But Roger was gone. Instead, Kevin stood there holding a long plastic tube.

"Hey Mickey, I hope you don't mind me telling you this, but I can see you are having a tough time with your anger."

Mickey the bulldozer was about to explode. He tried to pick up the drill with the razor-sharp blade, but his hands were sticky and he picked up handfuls of leaves and twigs and grass instead and couldn't shake them off.

"Usually, I would recommend anger management classes for you," Kevin taunted. "But I think we have to go softer on you." With that, he reached under the plastic tube next to him, pulled back a lever that loosened a spring that opened a bag, and thousands and thousands of white downy feathers rained down on Mickey, sticking to the honey covering him, and Mickey the bulldozer, Darth Vader, the scourge of the neighborhood, was turned into a big fat sticky chicken. Mickey struggled and thrashed the air with his arms and feathers flew everywhere, but all he could do was SQUAWK.

And as the *Wild Soccer Bunch* and Larry and even my
mom laughed and laughed, Mickey the chicken squawked
with fury and stumbled off, heading for the backyard
gate.

When Mickey finally made it to the gate, he was
stopped by Sox, who was guarding it. Sox bared his
fangs and growled. And Mickey, trying to stuff his
terror, turned in utter defeat, and slowly walked back
to Camelot.

We all waited for Mickey when he returned and
stopped dead in his tracks, right front of us.

I spoke first. "Strange how fast things change when

your friends aren't here to protect you." I was serious. "I'll take my money now. That will be $42.24 of my own money. And $221 that belongs to the *Wild Soccer Bunch*. No more, no less."

"Bubt," Mickey blurbled from under his honey and feather coating. Zoe went over and wiped the honey blocking his mouth since Mickey's arms, or wings, or whatever they were, weren't working very well. "Try it again, twerp," Zoe said.

"But, I don't have the money. I gave it to my cousin."

I stepped up to Mickey and got in his face. "Not our problem. Tell your gangster cousin winter came early. We don't care. Just bring us the money you stole from us. If you bring it, we won't rat you and your cousin out. Got that?"

I could see the noose tightening around Mickey. He looked one way – there we were. He looked the other – Sox growled at him.

"Okay, okay!" he said quickly, surrendering. "Give me four hours. Okay?"

I shrugged. I wasn't convinced. But we had to give him a chance to go get the money. We already knew his cousin was not going to be happy.

"Okay. Four hours. But what about your friends?" We all looked at what was left of the *Unbeatables*, stuck upside-down in trash cans. "Do you think they can wait four hours?

"I'll hurry!" Mickey said and stood there still looking at us dumbly like a giant *chicken nugget*.

"Well? What are you waiting for?" I asked. "The clock is ticking."

Mickey finally realized what was happening and ran off. But before he reached the gate, I called out to him.

"One more thing, Mickey!" I shouted.

Mickey cringed and a few downy white feathers blew off and floated around him.

"Don't ever let this happen again. Got that?"

Mickey nodded with dedication.

"Good!" I said. "We're soccer players. Not bullies."

Mickey nodded again, and then ran off. I turned to my friends.

"And that's the truth! All I want to do is go to school, and play for the *Wild Soccer Bunch*," I said, and hugged each and every one of them.

"All is well," I said. "As long as you're wild!" echoed the others. Then we went home to rest for our game in the *Devil's Pit*.

One More Secret

My mother brought Josh to bed first. It was after midnight but he was totally hyper and kept telling her the whole story over and over again about the honey and the feathers and how Mickey made a really bad bully, but a really good *chicken nugget*. She had to hear about the battle for Camelot at least four or five times, and she managed to laugh every time. Man, I love her so much! Do you know another mom who can watch a 10-ton jellyfish with a buzz-saw attack her own son and a monstrous creature from the prairie end up in a face-plant in our dog house? And laugh about it? She most definitely deserves my respect.

Having kissed Josh good night, she came to my room. She closed the door softly behind her and sat down on my bed right next to me. She looked at me quietly.

"Come on, ask already!" I thought, nervously twiddling with my toes underneath the blanket, grateful they weren't dislocated.

But my mother didn't have to ask. She knew I'd

understand her question without any words, and so I just blurted it out.

"I was looking for Dad."

My mother studied me for a long while.

"I know he lives in the Graffiti Towers!" I said, defending myself. "I don't even know him, Mom. I want to. And the Graffiti Towers is like the lost continent. Nobody knows anything about it!"

"Yeah, forget about the Northwest Passage or Outer Mongolia – or even Inner Mongolia," my mother replied with a twinkle in her eye. "The Graffiti Towers is the most undiscovered of them all."

I looked at my mom and she looked at me and both of us burst out laughing and hugged and I nuzzled into her. But then tears came down both our cheeks, at the same time.

"You're right, Julian. Your father lives in the Graffiti Towers," she whispered.

I held my breath. Suddenly I had an idea.

"Do you know Dad's email address?" My mother nodded.

"Will you scan this and send it to him?" I asked her hoarsely, and pulled a sheet of paper out from under my pillow.

My mother read the letter at least as often as Josh had told her the story of Honey and Feathers.

Father:

Would you please come to my soccer game? It's today in the Devil's Pit at 8 p.m. sharp. It's very important. I need you.

Your son, Julian

Julian Fort Knox, the all-in-one defender

"That's quite a mouthful that name of yours, Mr. all-in-one defender. What you did tonight was mighty heroic. How about we just call you *Julian the Mighty*?"

I couldn't believe she was saying this. What I meant to say was, I couldn't believe anyone would say anything so nice about me. "I love it," is what I said.

She stayed with me until I fell asleep and kissed me. One of her tears fell and landed on my cheek, and I felt it in my dream. It was a nice dream. We were all together again, mom and dad and me. At the big game.

While I was sleeping, Mickey the bulldozer came back. And he was not alone. Dressed as a giant chicken, he had caught the attention of the police. When they saw the traces of the battle for Camelot, he and the rest of the *Unbeatables* had to go to Juvenile Court. A judge sentenced them to six weeks of community service, working at an old folks' home. At first it was supposed to be twelve weeks, but when the police found out he had returned the money, they let them off easy. They also made Mickey and his friends go to a special class on bullying.

Larry took the money and went to the second-hand shop and bought himself a suit. He did it all by himself and he chose the one suit he thought would fit his position as the best coach in the world, the coach of the *Wild Soccer Bunch!*

Father:
Would you please come
to my soccer game? It's
today in the Devil's Pit
at 8 p.m. sharp.
It's very important.
I need you.
Your son, Julian
Julian Fort Knox,
the all-in-one defender

Star Shower

By late afternoon we were all up and out of bed. We could barely wait for the evening to roll around, and as soon as it was dark we ran off. Arriving at the *Devil's Pit* at the same time, we all stood in front of the gate. We were in awe.

The sign above the gate sparkled in the evening light, and for one magnificent moment the world was ours. It was a grand moment indeed as we stepped out onto the field wearing our *Wild Soccer Bunch* jerseys. The floodlights were on, bathing everything in a magical glow. In that grand moment we were dangerous and wild. Larry, dressed in his new pinstripe suit, proudly marched towards us, straightening his yellow and black and red tie.

It was an awesome moment. But like every awesome moment, this one was short lived. We were about to meet our match: *SC Ghosts United*.

Our opponents were already at the stadium when we arrived. They were all at least one year older and two

heads taller. They were giants!

"Hello! Finally!" Larry greeted us. "Welcome to the Eighth Dimension."

As if our opponents wanted to scare us into submission even before the game began, their left forward kicked the ball against the goal post so hard that even Alex the cannon Alexander was in awe.

Larry tried to give us confidence. "Men, they may be

bigger, but you are faster!" But that was little comfort. Actually, it was a lie!

The others were big all right, but we were by no means faster. We barely made it out of our own penalty box, and although Kyle, invincible as he is, stopped plenty of their shots, we were behind three zip by half-time. And I tell you, we were lucky it wasn't worse.

Larry was not happy. "You're playing like you left your confidence at home!" he complained. "Why are you all hanging back? Julian, you're enough to stop a team like this. What's up with you? Didn't you get enough sleep? Did you forget what we did last night? In case you forgot, I'll tell you. You all proved you can trust each other. So where is that trust out on the field? Julian! I'm talking to you. Two of those goals are on you!"

"1-2-3 WILD!" I barked my answer. That's how angry I was. Not with Larry. With myself. What Larry said was true, but he was wrong about the number. The third goal was my fault, too. I was anything but the all-in-one defender. I was anything but mighty. I was nothing but a tiny hole in a big block of Swiss cheese.

In the second half, I was constantly looking over to where my mother sat. She was by herself; my father had not shown up. If you want to know the truth, I was distracted and I was playing lousy. If I kept this up, we'd lose the first game in the *Devil's Pit* for sure. Our opponents had just scored a fourth goal, and one more time, I had set it up.

Embarrassed, I plucked the ball from the goal and kicked it to the center mark. My friends should not have saved me. My performance was not worth it. And I was so glad my dad hadn't seen I was the worst all-in-one defender ever!

The whistle blew. And that's when I saw him. My dad was standing at the corner of the field, right next to my mom. I knew it was my dad because he was standing in front of a very familiar pick-up truck. The driver who had mysteriously helped me three times was my dad!

I don't quite remember what happened after that. I was so happy. And I don't really know how what

happened, happened, but it did. Does that make sense? I'm sorry, my mind was racing and my heart was beating out of my chest, I was so excited. My father was there and in that magical moment, I knew we could not lose.

The whole team was energized. Tyler was our number 10 again and our mind-reader and intuition all rolled into one. He drove the ball across the field and played an unbelievable pass right to our opponent's goal area. Kevin, our slalom dribbler and star striker raced just in time to get the ball in and hit a mid-air volley, scoring our first goal of the game.

The next attack went over the right side. Danny raced past everyone, passed to Kevin who passed to the left to Joey the magician, who tricked defenders and finished with a great kick that sent the ball into the net. Two to four.

Tyler was up next. He dribbled from our own penalty box all the way to the opponent's goal and with the outside of his foot, he steered the ball into the upper right corner.

But three to four seemed to be it. The opponent's goal was slammed shut. Danny hit the post twice. Then suddenly Diego fought himself free five minutes before the end, whirled through the penalty box, heeled back to Kevin, who somehow got the ball into the net through a forest of legs.

Goal!!!

Kevin's fist represented us all. It said to everyone who was willing to listen, we weren't about to lose this game! We were wide awake and ready, but unfortunately the *SC Ghosts United* woke up, too.

Our opponents drove toward our goal as if it was the most important game of their lives. Well, it was actually, given they were all a year older, and a tie was too humiliating for them. But for us, a tie was a victory, so we summoned up all our strength and tried to hold off their attack. Even Kevin helped in the defense and threw himself into their right forward's shot, headed the ball over to me and I passed it on to Tyler. He kicked the ball forward. It was a first-class pass to Danny, the fastest midfielder in the world. He took off, and with that we had a chance to counter attack which was our chance to win. Fast as lightning we stormed ahead, but Danny lost the ball. Now the *SC Ghosts United* counter attacked. Their players were all faster than we were, and suddenly I was alone against two of their forwards. Only Kyle the invincible stood behind me.

They were double-passing and about to pass me by. I had to risk everything, and so I slid into the next pass and missed it by a hair. Kyle was by himself, but he was invincible. He threw himself into the shot like a brick wall with eyes and fisted the ball out of the penalty box.

Wow!

Now we really deserved the tie. The ref had the whistle in his hand already, when I noticed their midfielder. The ball rolled directly towards him; a great preparation for an easy volley. I looked at Kyle, but he was on the ground. He noticed the impending attack too late.

So I jumped up and while the number 10 of the *SC Ghosts United* hit the ball hard at the goal, I planted myself on the goal line, flew through the air, and thundered the ball out of and away from our penalty box.

Just as the referee whistled, the ball flew higher and

higher and finally hit one of the floodlights. It exploded and sparks showered down on us like stars.

TIE!! We didn't lose our first game in our very own stadium! I was exhausted but happier than ever. I stretched my arms as far and wide as I could.

Kevin, our star striker, and Zoe the fearless, ran over to me, wrapped their arms around me, and we bounced with joy! I looked up in the stands and there were my mother and father, on their feet, cheering wildly.

"Hey Julian Fort Knox, the all-in-one defender," Zoe shouted at me as the whole team surrounded me. "Your mom told us about your new name and we agree!"

That's when my mom and dad joined the *Wild Soccer Bunch* and Larry on the field. Kevin and Tyler lifted me up on their shoulders and my mom and dad joined in.

"Hurray for Julian the Mighty!" Zoe shouted.

And as the *Wild Soccer Bunch* and my parents carried me around the field, I knew exactly where I was, and where I belonged.

JOACHIM MASANNEK

Joachim was born in 1960 and studied German and Philosophy in college. He also studied at the University of Film and Television and worked as a camera operator, set designer, and screenwriter in films and television.

His children's book series *The Wild Soccer Bunch* has been published in 28 countries. As the screenwriter and director of the five *The Wild Soccer Bunch* movies, Joachim has managed to bring about nine million viewers into the theatres. He was the coach of the real *Wild Bunch Soccer* team and the father of two of the players, Marlon (Tyler) and Leon (Kevin).

JAN BIRCK

Jan was born in 1963 and is an illustrator, animation artist, art director, and cartoonist. Jan designs the *Wild Soccer Bunch* merchandising with Joachim. Jan lives in Munich with his wife, Mumi, and his soccer-playing sons, Timo and Finn.

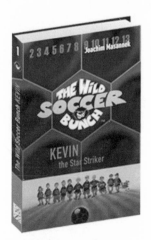

THE WILD SOCCER BUNCH
BOOK 1
KEVIN the Star Striker

When the last of the snow has finally melted, soccer season starts!

Kevin the Star Striker and the *Wild Soccer Bunch* rush to their field. They have found that Mickey the bulldozer and his gang, the *Unbeatables*, have taken over. Kevin and his friends challenge the *Unbeatables* to the biggest game of their lives.

Can the *Wild Soccer Bunch* defeat the *Unbeatables*, or will they lose their field of dreams forever? Can they do what no team has done before?

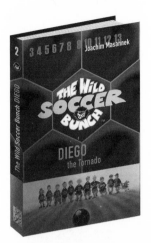

THE WILD SOCCER BUNCH
BOOK 2
DIEGO the Tornado

Fabio, the son of a famous Brazilian soccer player, wants to join the *Wild Soccer Bunch*. But Fabio's father has other plans. He makes his son play for the *Furies,* one of the best youth club teams in the country. The *Wild Soccer Bunch* is devastated, but Diego has a plan. He turns the *Wild Soccer Bunch* into a club team and challenges the *Furies* to a game! Can the *Wild Soccer Bunch* survive the game? Can their friendship endure the test?

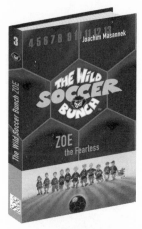

THE WILD SOCCER BUNCH
BOOK 3
ZOE the Fearless

Zoe is ten and soccer crazy. She spends each day dreaming of becoming the first woman to play for the U.S. Men's National Soccer Team. Her dad believes in her dream, and encourages her to join the *Wild Soccer Bunch*. Even though Zoe would be the only girl on the team, she knows she could be their best player. But the *Wild Bunch* is not open-minded when it comes to welcoming new teammates, especially when they are girls...

Zoe's dad has a plan. He organizes a birthday tournament and invites the *Wild Bunch*. They present Zoe with a pair of red high heels, expecting her to make a fool of herself during the tournament. Zoe gladly accepts her gift. She wears the heels during the biggest game of her life, and proves that she's got what it takes to be a wild, winning member of the *Wild Soccer Bunch*.

THE WILD SOCCER BUNCH
BOOK 5
MAX the Golden Boot

The championship game pits Max the golden boot and his team against the *Wild Soccer Bunch*. Max is so hooked by their attacking game that he dreams of being one of them. Although he is an amazing player, Danny and Kevin don't want him on the team. A power struggle ensues and threatens to break up and destroy the *Wild Soccer Bunch* who are on their top of their game.

The Wild Soccer Bunch
JUNIOR CHAMPIONS CLUB

Join the coolest club in the world!

Thank you for being a fan of the Wild Soccer Bunch!

You are invited to join our Junior Champions Club at:

www.wildsoccerbunch.com/jc

As a member of the Junior Champions Club, you get:

* The newest books in the series before everyone else!
* Rewards and prizes!
* Wild Soccer Bunch news and updates!
* And much more!

Love to read live to play!

Visit our web site for The Wild Soccer Bunch experience

Love to read, live to play!

WILD SOCCER PRESENTS:

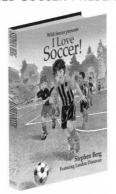

I LOVE SOCCER!

A must-have picture book that teaches
the basics of the game of soccer.
Includes a message from Landon Donovan!
Ages 3-6

AND ...

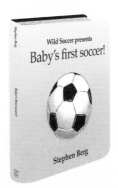

Baby's first soccer!

A great first introduction to the beautiful game of soccer.
Ages 1-3

Selected Reviews for Books 1, 2, and 3:

"The *Wild Soccer Bunch*, Book 1, is a mash-up of 'The Mighty Ducks' and 'The Seven Samurai' that every soccer mom will want on her child's reading list!"
—STEVEN E. de SOUZA, SCREENWRITER, 48 HOURS, DIE HARD

"A soccer-centric, middle-grade series that's been making waves abroad is arriving in the U.S. There are now more than nine million copies of the books in print in 32 countries."
—PUBLISHER'S WEEKLY

"This book is a clear winner."
—AMANDA RICHARDS, TOP AMAZON REVIEWER

"A great read for middle school students! I am a middle school librarian and the students absolutely love the first book in the series, "Kevin the Star Striker." There is nothing else like this series that I can find that is readable and appealing to the low and average middle school reader."
—C. THOMKA, SCHOOL LIBRARIAN

"A fun and exciting read for young soccer fans, *The Wild Soccer Bunch* is a top pick."
—MIDWEST BOOK REVIEW

"This is the kind of book that gets kids reading and begging their parents for the next book in the 13-book series."
—ROBIN LANDRY

"This is one of those books where you'll have a hard time putting it down; you will want to read the entire book once you start."

—SHAWN'S SHARINGS

"As a retired teacher, who has taught many reluctant readers, I highly recommend this inspiring book."

—EDUCATIONTIPSTER

"A shorter read, which means that even reluctant readers will not be intimidated. The story moves at a quick pace… Great humor… wonderful illustrations. My picky 9-year old said he would read more in the series (this is huge!!!)."

—AN EDUCATOR'S LIFE

"If your child goes to bed wearing soccer cleats so they won't miss one minute of field time in the morning, he or she will fall in love with the *Wild Soccer Bunch*."

—JENNYREVIEWS.COM

"This middle-grade novel isn't only fun and funny, it touches on some serious aspects of life."

—IMAGINATION-CAFE BLOG

"The writing is infectious and bodes well for a continuing series by this talented duo of Masannek and Brick."

—GRADY HARP, TOP AMAZON REVIEWER

"*The Wild Soccer Bunch* is at it again and their humorously exciting antics will thrill the young reader."

—D. FOWLER, AMAZON TOP 50 REVIEWERS, VINE VOICE

"Joachim Masannek's gift for finding the core of successful stories for youngsters is made even more pungent by the excellent and contributive illustrations by Jan Brick. They have found a niche and it looks like this rowdy but fun-loving soccer team is going to remain on field for years to come."

–GRADY HARP, AMAZON HALL OF FAME REVIEWER

"*Zoe the Fearless* will no doubt appeal to young readers, both boys and girls. There is lots of thrilling action for the tween reader along with some worthwhile moments highlighting interpersonal relationships and overcoming obstacles. The big print, line spacing, short chapters, and sporadic pictures make the book ideal for reluctant readers who get overwhelmed with many chapter books. I recommend *Zoe the Fearless* for ages 8-12."

–BOOKS 4 LEARNING

"This book is appropriate for an athletic child, aged 8-11, boy or girl, who is passionate about reading."

–LOCOMOTION OF EXPRESSION